THE FAILURE OF MULTICULTURALISM

SIMON LENNON

The Failure of Multiculturalism
Non-fiction
Immigration, Race Relations
A book in the collection: The West
A book in the series: Nationalism
Published by Pine Hill Books
Copyright © 2016, 2025 by Simon Lennon.
ISBN 978-1-925446-06-7 (electronic)
ISBN 978-1-925446-18-0 (paperback)
52,000 words, plus bibliography, references to 57,000 words
Cover image: Canberra, 2010

In memory of Tante Elaine

CONTENTS

1. WORDS

"We make mistakes because we are only human," said Ben Chifley, Australian prime minister, "and no political party can remake human nature." He died in 1951.

The multicultural West is trying to remake human nature. So did communist Eastern Europe.

"They believe in words," said Marek to my girlfriend and me in Warsaw, the first Thursday in November 1986. The worse things became, the better communists said things were. The less food people had to eat, the more they said harvests were plentiful.

Western Europe, North America, and Australasia have become the same. The lies we agree with, we call education. The facts we dislike, we call propaganda.

The overarching objective of our postmodern West is not the pursuit of knowledge, arts, fulfilment, or greatness, trying to build the best societies we can. Whether we like racial diversity or meekly accept what we feel powerless to prevent, we deploy an extraordinary amount of time, effort, and resources trying to make multiculturalism work.

Referring to culture when we mean race is among the West's new secrets of language. It's by no means the only one; we like keeping secrets. When culture sounds too much, we reduce it to cultural background. Multiculturalism is our euphemism for multiracialism.

"We believe one of Australia's greatest strengths is its cultural diversity," parliamentarian Malcolm Turnbull told Australian Broadcasting Corporation television in 2011, sounding like any number of Western leaders of their countries. His words were smart politics, making us happy when we so much need happiness. We're not so judgemental to adjudicate otherwise, or to examine homogenous nations elsewhere. Nor are we so rude as to ask why?

Before we chanted diversity, we preached tolerance, until we realised tolerance implied something unpleasant. So, we decided other races don't bring any ills. They bring only good, which we

1

should celebrate.

Since 1998, the Australian government has declared the twenty-first day of March each year to be Harmony Day. In the government's words (appearing on the official Harmony Day website in 2008), it *"is about bringing people together to celebrate Australia's community harmony, participation and cultural diversity."*

Posters, parades, and projects don't promote harmony. They insist it's already here. Six months after one Harmony Day and six months before the next, presumably as part of the annual Floriade spring flower show in September 2010, the flowers adorning a grassy Canberra park were shaped in huge letters: *"Harmony Day."* I couldn't stop thinking that if we really had such harmony, then we wouldn't need to keep saying we did.

My youngest daughter's year-one class at our local primary school needed to follow three sets of four rules each, the last of which was headed *"Respectful."* It went onto explain. *"We are respectful to each other when we"* do certain things including, as always, *"celebrate diversity."* Anything else was disrespectful.

On the wall at the rear of the classroom, the rules linked to photographs of the children's faces affixed to colourful cardboard figures holding hands. Celebrating diversity was the only rule upon which the teacher dwelt at the parent information evening three weeks into the school year. The children had spent two days discussing it.

At the end of the first week of fourth term 2011, my wife and I were at the school to see our second son receive a banner and our youngest daughter receive a merit award. By then, all three sets of school rules were displayed in white letters from large black boards at one end of the school basketball court and play area.

Ernie Friedlander, a survivor of the Jewish Holocaust through World War II, neatly summarised the purpose behind Harmony Day. In 2005, he started a poster and song writing competition that, in 2011, involved two hundred and fifty-seven schools across New South Wales. "I wanted to overcome prejudice, discrimination, and stereotyping," he explained, "and in the process, plant the seed into the minds of young people to identify and realise not to be judgemental of people, rather to consider them on their merit."

Judgement is a rational assessment having regard to all available information. Merit means seeing only the good.

We see people through the prisms of our heartfelt ideals, with a teary-eyed glee at how happy we are. We talk as if talking makes anything real, demanding affirmations from others. It's the essence of Harmony Day.

Six thousand, three hundred, and seventy students produced posters and songs espousing harmony in Friedlander's 2011 competition. "Each student who has created an artwork gets a certificate of participation posted to school," said Friedlander. In true postmodern style, "everyone is basically a winner." Entrants needed only to say we had harmony to win.

Funnily enough, the theme that year was "making our world a better place," in a rare implication the world could be improved. I'm not sure many of the posters or songs dwelt upon that, except to say we make the world better by accepting more immigrants.

Our exertions don't end with Harmony Day. My children, like thousands of other primary school children across New South Wales, participated each year in the Multicultural Perspectives Public Speaking Competition.

The competition, said the 2009 notice, "*aims to heighten awareness of multicultural issues among primary school students while developing their interest and skills in public speaking, as well as their confidence.*" Such aims were high and noble for children so young, except that no parent or child doubted the awareness required of them. The topics that year included such pointed ones as "*When does a migrant become an Australian?*" and "*Welcoming refugees.*"

According to the notes under the heading for evaluation in the 2013 competition, speeches "*need to show an understanding of multiculturalism.*" That meant they had to endorse it. This was no forum to wonder whether immigrants ever became Australians or opportunity to review the West's open borders. It wasn't even a place for public speaking. Abraham Lincoln's *Gettysburg Address* would fail a multicultural speaking competition for failing to laud racial diversity, but three grunts would suffice if two of them were "dumb" and "racism."

Students also "*need to display a balance of humour and sincerity,*" meaning they must believe what they say. When we reward people for believing what we want them to believe, they believe, or at least pretend to believe.

Sincerity is profoundly important in our postmodern, multicultural West. We have to learn how to fake it.

The only imagination we require is finding new ways of saying the same things: how much we like other races around us; how awful things used to be. The words don't have to be true. They have to be right. Scrutinising what people say more than anything they do, words previously unimportant have become all-important, to people without anything innovative or profound to declare.

We're telling children what to believe, to the point of pressing them to say it aloud, rather than leaving them to learn from their experiences or the experiences of others. If our children don't like multiculturalism, they don't learn public speaking. They don't develop confidence. We don't want people questioning multiculturalism able to address a crowd. We don't want them feeling confident.

Ten years old in 2009, my second daughter picked what she thought was the easiest topic for her speech: *"What comes after saying 'sorry'?"* Unfortunately, she assumed the topic was civility. With pretty colours and diverse writing styles, she prepared a speech about forgiveness, noting several responses a civil person might make to an apology: *"Please"*, *"Yes, please"*, *"Thank you"*, *"Yes thank you"*, *"That's alright."*

Her teacher told her to redraft it. The topic referred specifically to our supposed past cruelty to Aborigines; white racial guilt doesn't contemplate forgiveness. Like the topic *"Reconciliation and me,"* the only speech my daughter could make was about more things white Australia could do to help Aborigines. If such topics help white children build confidence, then it is to apologise more confidently.

I couldn't fault my daughter for her error. After all, that was the Multicultural Perspectives Public Speaking Competition. It wasn't the annual Sorry Day.

My daughter chose a different topic altogether. She spoke, truthfully or not, of *"Who are we and where are we going."*

My eldest daughter, turning twelve later that year, told me that all she'd learnt at primary school about the Aborigines was the genocide she was told we'd committed against them. It wasn't true. Like Marek with his children, I corrected her.

It doesn't end with primary school. My eldest daughters' high school had no lockers for the children's books and bags (because past lockers concealed drugs) until my second daughter's final year (when it installed them for younger years), but convened

Multicultural Day annually. Normal classes were suspended, but not for talk of challenges or problems when races live side by side. Instead, rooms blissfully promoted immigration with food aplenty.

My eldest daughter's history assignment at the start of first term in 2011 asked the children to contrast European colonisation of Australia with that of America, examining war, disease, and massacres. There was no consideration of Europeans on our merits, no need to be respectful by celebrating that diversity. The diversity we applaud when other races come is one we condemn when we look back to the years white people came. Refusing to consider positive or even neutral consequences of European colonisation, the only consequences contemplated were strikingly negative.

The assignment contrasted with the topics for the multicultural speaking competition distributed at the same time to our youngest children by their primary school. Refusing to imagine negative or neutral consequences of interracial immigration, the only consequences contemplated were strikingly positive.

The first arrivals supposedly suffered for our coming. The last arrivals supposedly improved our lots. We're the arrivals in between. Colonial Europeans become indebted to immigrants, but remain indebted to indigenous peoples. While we presume modern-day immigrants all become Australians, we presume European colonists never became Australians. Europeans coming was an absolute evil. Everyone else coming is an absolute good. While we only entertain consideration of the supposed benefits of other people's immigration, our forebears enjoy no such luxury.

(What's never clear through our ideologies of immigration is whether multiracial immigration ameliorates indigenous peoples' suffering. When, late in the 1980s or so, Aboriginal leader Charles Perkins expressed concern for the impact of Asian immigration on indigenous Australians, we shouted him down. The chorus condemning him said a victim of white people's racism, as everyone of another race is presumed to be, shouldn't tolerate other people being victims. I never heard an indigenous leader dare express such concern again.)

Among all the films my eldest son's year-ten English class could have studied, the school chose *Mississippi Burning*, a fictionalised account of the murder by white people of two Jews and a black man campaigning for black American rights in 1964. Student assignments required more discussion of white people's prejudice. My son had learnt well. He topped his form for his work, with the advantage in knowing to talk of the evils of racism.

Other parents tell similar tales. My friend Tim's son Sam at his school studied a unit on anti-Semitism. It wasn't about Jews or Muslims, but about us in our bad old days.

Children know little of the world, except as others describe it. So do most adults. From our schools come our adults.

With all I'd observed of my children's schooling, I was intrigued by one person's response to the uproar following an appearance by John Elliott, a former president of the Carlton Football Club and of the Liberal Party, on the television programme *Can Of Worms* in 2011. Elliott was part of a panel answering the question, "Should we acknowledge traditional owners at official events?" The traditional owners were Aborigines, not us.

Acknowledging them was "sheer bloody nonsense," said Elliott. "I was in St Paul's Cathedral the other day and there's the dean of the church, and all he did for the first five minutes was talk about the abos. Indigenous people, sorry. Not allowed to say that word."

Panellist Maude Garrett pulled him up for his language.

"That's how we were grown up and talked about them," replied Elliott, "but I know it's changed and I'm sorry for that." Elliott was born in 1941.

Elliott's apologies weren't enough. Among the two hundred and twenty-five comments posted to the *Age* newspaper website by the time the next day I read the article reporting Elliott's remark, one was particularly interesting. *"Clearly it is offensive,"* wrote Sarah, *"but that is how Australians were raised to consider Indigenous Australians in the past. If you read children's books from the early half of the 20th century you will find extremely offensive and racist views and terms. Such as that Indigenous Australians were "dying out", and judgments on blood percentages etc. My father was similarly raised and also uses the term on occasion. We can only encourage those who were indoctrinated in this way to change their language, and be confident that such language is not part of how younger non-Indigenous Australians think of Indigenous Australians."*

The kindest words we can say of our forebears are that they didn't know any better: that they would've been like us if they'd known what we know. We grant them the presumption of ignorance.

"While it does not excuse it," Sarah continued, *"a perhaps more*

troubling aspect of his comments is his problem with traditional owners being acknowledged rather than the term itself, which was common parlance up until several decades ago. I would say he'd not be unusual among people of his age group in this usage."

Generalisations by people's age no longer surprised me; they're the norm in a way that racial and religious generalisations no longer are. What surprised me were Sarah's presumptions about indoctrination. Elliott's generation was among the last to grow up free to speak much as people felt and to say what they thought to be true, without fearing others virulently feeling offence. Theirs was a time people abbreviated words with colourful turns of phrase we curtail.

When we of the West lived in harmony, before becoming mindlessly immersed in idiot slogans, we had no need for Harmony Day. We had no need to declare we were happy, when we really were happy. Not trying so hard to convince ourselves that the present was wonderful, we had no need to denigrate our past.

My generation followed Elliott's generation. No one taught us to be racist. No school indoctrinated us to value our culture and race, forming judgements about ours and others. I never heard anyone being reviled when discrimination was the norm as I heard people speaking out of turn being reviled by 2011.

Of course, people could've been indoctrinated without realising it; education is easier than re-education. *"Men are born ignorant, not stupid,"* wrote English philosopher Bertrand Russell in 1945, *"they are made stupid by education."* Our potted lives are products of our times and places.

When we're not trying to change people, we're managing them. We've made race and religion relevant whenever mentioning them promotes racial or religious diversity. They're irrelevant whenever mentioning them doesn't. We control what we say, but we have to do that. Our countries might blow apart if we don't.

We used to say truth was the first casualty of war. It's certainly the first casualty of multiculturalism.

A handful of journalists, academics, and other commentators tucked away report facts that don't find their way into multicultural speaking competitions. People I've met revealed similar experiences to mine. Many more people surely could too. Instead of Harmony Day, we could do something bold. For one day of the year, at least, we could tell the truth. Imparting information and knowledge, protecting people, we could have Honesty Day.

In Sarah's sense of enlightenment, so intriguing wasn't her presumption that past generations must've been indoctrinated to think as they thought. It was her presumption that hers hadn't been.

2. HUBRIS

In a 2013 essay 'A Plea for Caution From Russia' about the Syrian civil war published in the *New York Times* newspaper, President Vladimir Putin warned Americans of the dangers of any people seeing *"themselves as exceptional, whatever the motivation."* At the time, unrelated to his essay, Russia was expending huge sums of money subsidising her North Caucasus, trying to prevent racial and religious tensions pulling the Russian Federation apart.

The multicultural West thinks we're exceptional, able to create multiracial societies nobody else has. Suggesting everything isn't peachy among a multitude of races would be a gruesome, bleak thing to do. Talking about race and reality can seem churlish and nasty to people happily unaware, inviting them to consider matters too horrible to contemplate. Even the most rudimentary questioning of our supposed success would be racist; we refuse to be racist.

Letting go of our ideals can be as hard as indigenous races find letting go of their countries. Believing only what we say are the benefits of multiculturalism, we'd rather wallow in a broken hovel than think we're wrong, or just ordinary. We smile and laugh, never wondering what might be coming closer.

Driving to work at TNT Shipping & Development Limited through the late 1980s or early '90s, approaching a roundabout through suburban Leichhardt, I slowed. A red car veered from the kerb into the road in front of me. Our cars would have collided, but I braked suddenly. I sounded my horn.

The red car stopped. The outraged driver leapt out. A young Middle Eastern man with swarthy olive skin and black hair spat a thick splash of spit towards me.

The reason he hated me didn't matter. Hating me didn't matter. What mattered was his capacity to harm me, and that horrible thick slab of spit on my windscreen. I thrust my foot on the accelerator and sped around him. He leapt back into his car and sped after me.

His car reached mine and continued until it was beside me.

With both our cars speeding forward, he thrust his arm out the open window beside him, holding a baseball bat he tried furiously to strike at my car.

I again pulled away, to where I could see the registration plate of his car. We became caught in just enough traffic for me to grapple with a pen and paper and scribble the letters and numbers of his car registration plates, before again he drove near me. In two speeding cars, I held up my pen and paper so his eyes saw what I'd done as surely as I saw his angry face so close to me. He braked and turned sharply into the next side street. I memorised the names of the manufacturer and model of his car.

A short walk from my place of work was Redfern police station, where I reported the incident. The registration plates were from a stolen car: not the car to which the plates had been affixed that morning. The policeman said he could do nothing more. I filed a report, in case the registration plates appeared in a robbery or other crime, but never heard again from the police about it. I didn't think much again about the crime that wasn't committed against me, until writing what became this book.

The third Wednesday in March 2009, I took my second son and another boy to our municipal swimming pool. I remarked to the man tending the counter that the pool was a tranquil place, under the gum trees. He replied, "Not when the Lebanese come along."

"We're not meant to say that," I told him. "We meant just to say how great it is that they're here."

Sam "The Assassin," leader of the Middle Eastern street gang Asesinoz M.C., objected to prejudice against Lebanese. "There are a handful of good Australians but most are racist by assuming Lebanese people are responsible for all crime," he said in 2009, not considering himself Australian. "When they see a Middle Eastern walking down the street they assume they are Lebanese. I am half Lebanese and half Iraqi, but I want the public and the police to know this: Don't forget about the Persians, Iraqis, Afghanis, Turks etc. …because they do crimes too. That is why we have posted these videos up." He'd distributed films about other Middle Eastern and South Asian criminals so we'd not think so poorly of Lebanese.

So much as drawing a negative inference about people of another race, thinking they're anything but good (save only for that handful of individuals not as bad as we can be anyway), we dismiss for being irrational: another of our postmodern phobias. We haven't a word for rationally feeling heightened anxieties about other races in general or particular, certain such fears can never be rational. A woman sitting in an otherwise empty carriage can't let the race of the man coming towards her influence her decision whether to prime her telephone for a call or to guide her fingers nearer the can of mace in her bag.

Eight Middle Eastern men arrived in two cars at a party at Kintore Street, Wahroonga the first Friday in October 2009, where they were refused entry. They began harassing a young man outside. When sixteen-year-old Luke Fogarty went to his friend's aid, the Middle Easterners broke Fogarty's nose and his jaw in two places. A week later, doctors didn't know if Fogarty's nerve damage would ever heal.

That same day, the accountant at Golden Cross Resources Limited told me of a person he knew waiting at a bus stop in Epping, when a carload of Middle Eastern men pulled up. A few leapt out and attacked him. Carl said no newspaper reported the assault; we don't draw attention to their crimes. Being interesting doesn't make something newsworthy.

After telling a meeting of young members of her Christian Democratic Party in Potsdam on the middle Saturday of October 2010 that immigrants remained welcome in Germany, Chancellor Angela Merkel admitted that attempts to create a multicultural society "and to live side by side and to enjoy each other...has failed, utterly failed." She wanted immigrants to learn to speak German.

Turkey's Prime Minister Recep Tayyip Erdogan rejected assimilation for the three million Turks living in Germany. He told the German newspaper *Bild* (in an interview published the second Wednesday of February 2011) that requiring Turks to speak German before moving to Germany denied them their human rights. Immigration to the West had become a human right, at least for Turks, as it was not outside the West.

There's no reason why people should change their behaviours from one place to live in another, even if we graciously ask them to do so. When they fail, we indulge them by saying they're not used to our ways. When their children make the same failings, we blame our schools and society. Without notions of race to distinguish them from our sons and daughters, we blame all of us together.

In his 2011 speech 'What makes multiculturalism great is

mutual respect,' Australian immigration minister Chris Bowen blamed Europeans for the failure of multiculturalism there. "Many countries in Europe have nations within nations: significant communities living 'parallel lives,' perpetuating segregation based on ethnic, religious, or cultural divides... Australian governments...have tried to instil a sense of belonging in Australia while encouraging the participation of all people... It seems to me, if you accept the benefits of a diverse population, you then have a choice: do you respect, embrace and welcome the cultures of those you have invited to make Australia home or do you shun them?" Europe *had* respected, embraced, and welcomed her immigrants. Bowen presumed the only thing wrong with multiculturalism is the white people.

"Do you invite their full participation or do you treat them as guest workers and hope they integrate," asked Bowen, targeting Germans, "while all along suspecting they won't?"

Bowen insisted there was goodness inside immigrants' heads, while claiming insight into supposed suspicions inside European heads. How those secret suspicions, which no German revealed to me, created racial and other divisions wasn't obvious.

Bowen criticised Germany for not handing out citizenship to immigrants, as other Western countries had. A Scotsman in conversation with me at our family's Uniting church in 2013 thought Germans were being unfair because, said Craig, our Volkswagen was most likely made by a Turk, but Germany suffered fewer problems with immigrants than other countries did.

That might've been due to her police and security forces, but Germany still had problems. In 2015, a confidential police report leaked to *Der Spiegel* magazine warned of districts in Duisburg where immigrant gangs took over entire trains. Duisburg was home to sixty thousand mostly Turkish Muslims along with Sinti and Roma gypsies in a total population of half a million.

Aside from their community leaders and other spokespeople playing politics, we're more upset about bad impressions of other races than they are. In May 2013, two white women on the Cable News Network were appalled at what they believed might've been the most racist commercial ever filmed. It portrayed a white woman identifying the assailant who'd beaten her from a police line-up of black Americans and a goat; the goat was the cool one. Mountain Dew had intended the commercial to appeal to black males, not white women. The musician making the commercial recognising that black men beat white women was Tyler, The Creator: a black man.

The mobs frightening Philadelphians through 2009, 2010, and 2011 didn't attract much news. When they did, they were faceless flash mobs. They might've remained so, had the mayor Michael Nutter not told the marauding black youths: "You have damaged your own race."

We could've joked about the mayor's name had he been white. We don't joke about other races. Nutter was black.

Nutter wasn't the only black man flouting our racial sensitivities. The mayor's words "took courage," said the head of Philadelphia's chapter of the National Association for the Advancement of Coloured People, Whyatt Mondesire. "These are majority African American youths, and they need to be called on it."

Late paragraphs in the news report of Nutter's comments mentioned that flash mobs had also stormed Milwaukee (which had fallen far from being the 1950s setting of the television series *Happy Days*) and the District of Columbia, the seat of American government. It included a file photograph from the third Saturday in March 2010, of thousands of black people running down South Street, Philadelphia.

The *Chicago Tribune* newspaper reported mobs carrying out five random attacks on people in broad daylight in Chicago in June 2011 (drawing my attention to Chicago as corruption trials never had). "The next thing I know is I'm being hit by the helmet, then being dragged into the street," said insurance salesman Krzysztof Wilkowski. "I couldn't believe it. It was broad daylight outside, there were people around, and this happened." The text mentioned a victim from Japan. The photograph was of a white victim and black assailants.

We only care if money's at stake. "There are economic consequences if people think downtown isn't safe," said city alderman Brendan Reilly, concerned about the impact of violence upon tourism and convention business.

Reading the report through the newspaper's website, the usual space for readers' comments was missing. *"The board for this story has been closed because of excessive violations of the Tribune's comment policies,"* it explained.

Those policies were detailed below. *"Constructive and respectful comments related to the topic of the story are welcome; abusive, crass or vulgar comments are not. Comments containing vulgar words will be filtered out. Please make sure your language is civil and your comment furthers the conversation. Personal attacks on others who comment are not appropriate. Hateful, racist or threatening comments are not allowed.... Ignoring the standards will result in your comment being removed. Repeat offenders will be banned. If warranted, we will take down entire comment boards."*

Chicago police superintendent Garry McCarthy told parishioners at St Sabina Church "everybody's afraid of race," but not him. His complaint wasn't with black men attacking white people and Asians, but with a line of history: "Slavery, segregation, black codes, Jim Crow." He blamed the Chicago attacks not on the criminals' race but "government-sponsored racism," namely, "Federal gun laws that facilitate the flow of illegal firearms into our urban centres across this country that are killing our black and brown children." (The deaths of white children seem not to have interested him.)

A black president didn't diminish his perception that American governments were white, pulling black fingers on the triggers of guns. McCarthy called for "recognition of who's paying the price for the gun manufacturers being rich and living in gated communities."

After Neighbourhood Watch patrolman George Zimmerman killed black teenager Trayvon Martin in a gated community in Sanford, Florida in February 2012, *Associated Press* labelled Zimmerman white, but he wasn't. Somebody coined the term "white Hispanic" to describe Hispanics who kill, even in self-defence.

None of it fazes us, in our merry middle-class homes. Ours is the ecstasy in virtual space people must feel when they're high on hallucinogenic drugs. The challenge is waking up in the morning.

White man Dave Forster and Iranian woman Marjon Rostami stopped their car at traffic lights in Norfolk, Virginia one Saturday night in April 2012, when a black teenager threw a rock at their car. A hundred black teenagers attacked them, taking turns to punch and kick them. The local newspaper, the *Virginian-Pilot*, didn't report the crime, in spite of the victims being newspaper employees.

Norfolk police were similarly nonplussed. "It's what they do," said one officer, referring to the teenagers in public housing who congregate on weekends.

The day after the beatings, Forster searched the Twitter website for mention of them. "*I feel for the white man who got beat up at the light*," wrote one person.

"*I don't*," wrote another, indicating laughter. "*(do it for trayvon martin)*"

While the media obsessed with Martin's death more than seven hundred miles away, the attack on Forster and Rostami took two weeks to reach the news, and then only because of an opinion piece. "*How can we change it if we don't know about it?*" asked columnist Michelle Washington. "*How can we make it better if we look away?*"

Our right of free speech is the right not to report, not to mention matters we consider distasteful. Information is selective, shirking away from reality bits we don't like.

Rhetoric can't replace reality. It can only conceal or reveal it. We can't talk our way out of reality by touting a stream of evidence we like and denying evidence we don't. Saying people are the same doesn't change the differences.

We presume to make multiracialism work by preventing white prejudice, as if prejudice is the problem we face. We pretend we've no problems around race, so there's none to solve. It frees up our time to deal with other people's problems. It's the arrogance of our ignorance, basking in our accolades while strangers tear us down. Problems aren't resolved by being ignored.

3. WARNINGS

When radio station *Granskning Sverige* in 2015 asked the *Aftonposten* and *Expressen* newspapers whether they felt any responsibility to warn Swedish women to stay away from certain men more likely to rape them, the journalists were deeply offended. One journalist asked why that should be a journalist's responsibility?

Multiculturalism depends upon white people's disregard for other white people's well-being: our individualism. Our compatriots are lives like ours, but we don't care if all of them suffer or die provided we don't discriminate. We'll protect women from white men, but not from men of other races.

We'll protect other races. After a mentally retarded man, Isais Vasquez, was beaten with a shovel or axe handle in February 2013, requiring medical personnel to insert fourteen stitches to close his wound, police and volunteers warned Hispanic residents in Plano, Texas of five violent attacks on Hispanic men walking alone. Hispanics carried cash instead of using banks and those illegally in America feared coming to the attention of authorities by reporting crime. The attackers were two or three young black men.

Along with Basque separatists and Muslim terrorists, the American Department of State in 2009 was concerned about Spanish police. It warned travellers that "*racist prejudices could lead to the arrest of Afro-Americans who travel to Spain.*"

Fifteen months on, in August 2010, the warning didn't deter the black American president's wife Michelle Obama and their daughter Sasha, along with forty friends, from a summer holiday in the Villa Padierna Palace Hotel on the Costa del Sol. Admittedly, a corps of bodyguards would protect them if the two hundred and fifty Spanish officers and military police, divers, bomb disposal experts, and dog handlers assigned to protect them arrested them.

Their visit led to the State Department's warning reaching the attention of Spanish journalists, who considered it offensive. The warning was removed.

Other races care for their race. The September 2016 edition of

Air China's in-flight magazine *Wings of China* warned travellers, *"London is generally a safe place to travel, however precautions are needed when entering areas mainly populated by Indians, Pakistanis and black people."*

Readers' comments to the *Sun* newspaper said the warning was warranted. Josh Kellaway said a few policemen warned him not to enter London suburbs like Harlesdon and Brixton as long ago as 1986. "Of course," they said, "we'll deny it if we're quoted."

Nevertheless, parliamentarian Rosena Allin-Khan insisted the warning "is not reflective of London at all." She called it "offensive to all Londoners, not just the ethnic minorities mentioned."

We've made words more important than people: our people. *"Racism hurts everyone,"* insisted a topic for years three and four in the 2011 multicultural speaking competition at our local primary school, available to my sons aged eight and nine. It wasn't true. Our rejection of racism hurts.

Withholding facts from children for their sake, knowing the day will come they'll be old enough for truth, allows children their childhoods: imaginations of a world that never was, in visions better for being unreal. Denying them reality for our sake, casting visions becoming dangerous for being untrue, is child abuse. We inculcate our children with our ideals for what we wish the world was. They listen faithfully unaware the truth is something else, hidden far beyond our smiles.

Following Trayvon Martin's death, black Americans like Cosby Hunt and Corey Dade spoke of the advice black American parents give their teenage sons to survive racism in America. What quickly became known as the Talk included suggestions like never leaving a store without a shopping bag (so storekeepers know they're not thieves) and not loitering outside (because police looking for criminal suspects focus on young, black, male loiterers). White Americans talked of the Talk as more evidence of the persistent problem of racism.

In response, British-born journalist John Derbyshire (whose wife was Chinese) wrote of a version of the Talk for parents who aren't black in an article for *Taki's* magazine. *"If accosted by a strange black in the street,"* he wrote, *"smile and say something polite but keep moving."* (It was among two dozen suggestions I should have read before visiting Baltimore.) *"If you are white or Asian and have kids, you owe it to them to give them some version of the talk. It will save them a lot of time and trouble spent figuring things out for themselves. It may save their lives."*

Derbyshire was also contributing editor for the *National Review*, whose editor Rich Lowry called Derbyshire's article "nasty and indefensible." It fired him.

Warning black children about other people's racism is socially acceptable. Warning other people's children about black crime isn't. Protecting our children's lives demands we ensure they act safely, knowing where the risks of harm most likely lie, but we're to do so paying no regard to race. We demonise discrimination and carry on regardless, in spite of dangers that make prejudice desirable.

George Zimmerman's trial would reveal black people's racial epithet "cracka" to describe white people, especially the poor of the American South. Slang terms by which other races deride us aren't normally reported.

"My parents grew up during the age of busing and public housing in the Northeast," commented Il Barone following criticisms of Derbyshire's article. *"It was a nightmare for whites. There was gang violence in schools and on the streets. My mother was mugged walking out of mass, no less... My parents did the right thing and moved to a town that is 95% white, so I could be raised in better conditions than they were raised in."*

It was history I'd never before heard. I'd heard only of racist white people moving away from incoming blacks.

"Nothing in all the world is more dangerous than sincere ignorance and conscientious stupidity," wrote black American churchman Martin Luther King, Junior in his 1963 book *Strength to Love*. We prefer ignorance and stupidity to racism.

Our conspiracy of silence condemns people to harm. No schoolchild's speech about poor refugees would've mentioned six Australian customs officers contracting potentially fatal tuberculosis from their contact with asylum seekers in 2009 and '10. The infections came to light not in any discussion about refugees, but in a wage dispute between the Community and Public Sector Union and the Australian Customs and Border Protection Service.

In 2010, an Australian senate committee heard that twenty cases of tuberculosis had been detected in immigration detention centres over an eleven-month period. One detainee had tested positive to typhoid. A further eleven had hepatitis B. Three fell ill with chicken pox. (If a schoolchild's speech mentioned them, then it's because they're reasons to help them.)

Extolling the wonderful things immigrants bring to the West doesn't touch upon disease. Maligning past European colonialism does.

In 2013, an American government moratorium on deporting illegal immigrant children led to a surge in unaccompanied minors entering America. Department of Homeland Security inspector general John Roth sent secretary Jeh Johnson a memorandum dated the penultimate day of July 2014 saying that many unaccompanied alien children "*and family units require treatment for communicable diseases, including respiratory illnesses, tuberculosis, chicken pox, and scabies.*" The American government transported them around the country, without being so discriminatory or disrespectful as to screen their health.

Prevalent in Latin America but rarely seen in America before 2013, enterovirus D-68 causes paralysis like polio and 'flu symptoms. In September 2014, the Center for Disease Control reported that the virus had reached epidemic levels in Colorado, Illinois, Iowa, Kansas, Kentucky and Missouri. "*The United States is currently experiencing a nationwide outbreak of enterovirus D68 (EV-D68) associated with severe respiratory illness,*" it reported in October.

The centre denied any link between the epidemic and illegal immigrant children. If so, then the events were astoundingly coincident. "Keep in mind that Latin American children likely have some immunity and may not be sick, while still contagious," pointed out Jane Orient of the Association of American Physicians and Surgeons.

The most infamous of infectious diseases remains the human immunodeficiency virus causing acquired immunodeficiency syndrome, AIDS, passed through bodily fluids. Our slogans insist the often-lethal virus doesn't discriminate and thus neither should we. News reports in 2011 didn't mention the race of John Choul Chan from Findon in Adelaide when he pleaded guilty to sleeping with women while knowing he carried the virus. A report did, however, mention he sought leave to travel to Sudan to visit his mother.

Godfrey Zaburoni knew he was carrying the virus when he slept with hundreds of Australian women, including a girlfriend in Sydney. She was presumably among the list of twelve names he gave police. News reports in 2010 described him as being a circus acrobat, without meaning to be funny, and mentioned he'd been born in Zimbabwe. Photographs of him standing bare chested made his race unmistakeable.

During my two periods working in Finland in 1996 and '97, Thomas referred to the widely reported story of a rare American in Helsinki, who carried the human immunodeficiency virus and could have infected up to two hundred Finnish women. Caring so much for his people, Thomas was dismayed so many Finnish women had slept so freely with a stranger. Having trusted all they'd read in newspapers and magazines and all they'd seen in films and on television, they'd ne'er be racially prejudiced against anyone. The contagious American, unnamed, was black.

Rumour suggested black heterosexual men were far more likely than white heterosexual men to carry the virus, but we weren't having a bar of racism. Nor were we so racist as to imagine black men being indifferent to white women's lives, although white people weren't rushing to protect them. Racism might've saved them from the virus but we'd rather be bashed, raped, or murdered, or at least let other people be bashed, raped, or murdered, than be racist. Treating the black American as no less a victim of the virus than those women, we do what we do without caring about consequences.

Quietly, in another conversation, Thomas told me he thought Finns were glad the country hadn't accepted immigrants as had other Western countries. Without them, Finns were wealthy, without the much-vaunted energies and stresses of multiculturalism. Swedes and other foreign residents neither felt nor gave offence; Finns were the indigenous peoples. We, of course, would find reasons other than race for the safe streets of Finland, such as the cold weather or monetary richness, although Sweden was just as cold and rich but no longer safe.

The *Daily Telegraph* newspaper published a warning to farmers from New South Wales police about a group of fifty confidence tricksters in October 2008. Mentioning the fifty were Irish gypsies might've been a special exemption from our rules for not reporting race because we don't realise gypsies are a race, or because they're gypsies. Apparently more concerned about maligning gypsies than warning farmers, the *Sydney Morning Herald* newspaper didn't report the warning, at least that I saw.

Victorian Police avoid racial descriptions, but are comfortable with geographical origins. "We believe overseas crime gangs from Eastern Europe are preying on Victorians," warned police officer Terry Ryan in July 2010. Police had identified twenty-eight automatic teller machines in greater Melbourne with false card entry points and panels hiding tiny cameras above the keyboard to capture cardholders' personal identification numbers. I wondered if gypsies were tarnishing Eastern Europe's reputation.

In 2011, the New South Wales Department of Fair Trading released a detailed profile of gypsy crime gangs. "They prey on the vulnerable," warned police officer Trent Atkins, "and are cunning thieves."

I wonder what other hurt could be avoided with racism. If some races are more criminal than others, then the people blithely trusting them aren't naïve. They're victims of our cruel and culpable propaganda.

German student Julius G campaigned for open borders and protested against Germans concerned about Muslim immigration. While waiting for two friends outside a pizzeria in Neustadt, Dresden, the middle Saturday in October 2015, six to eight North African men attacked him, stabbing him, without stealing anything from him. Feeling "very sad," he had no idea why they attacked him.

All our lauding of immigration and racial integration can't detract from the fact there'd be white people alive and unharmed if we'd not allowed other races to come. We're more interested in the immigrants and their children whose lives are better and might have been saved because we did. They're the people upon whom we pride ourselves, without seeing our bloody hands for crimes they commit. Our embrace of racial and religious diversity matters more than human life, even thousands or millions of human lives, even our own.

Every instance we learn a raceless criminal isn't white, we have cause to wonder if personal security demands we watch warily that darker-skinned stranger in a black leather jacket (like the one I sometimes wear) rather than inviting him home. Not everyone is willing to be a martyr for multiculturalism: dying knowing she's not racist in the people against whom she takes precautions. Racial and religious discrimination might save people's lives. Not being racially and culturally truthful might be killing people.

I can say with confidence that the only times in my life I've been a victim of crime and known the perpetrator's race, he wasn't white. (That might change after publication of this book.)

Stephen Hagan established his credentials as a crusader against racism by leading a decade-long battle to rename the E.S. "Nigger" Brown Pavilion at the Toowoomba Sports Ground. Nigger had been Brown's popular nickname, in a long-past era where people didn't care so much about language as we've come to care. Hagan's bid failed in the Federal Court and High Court, but the United Nations said the word should be removed. It remained there for another five years before the state government insisted it go in 2008. Empowered by that success, Hagan complained about Coon cheese.

Hagan was Aboriginal, an Aborigine of the Year no less. As a University of Southern Queensland academic, he told a forum on reducing violence in indigenous families in Mackay in 2009 that he refused to lend Aborigines money. He banned them from his home to protect his son and daughter from abuse.

Prejudice can be rational, based upon knowledge and experience. Trust can be irrational, based upon ignorance and misconception.

4. CRITICAL ANALYSIS

The last Tuesday evening in July 2010, I attended my first alumni debate of the Macquarie Graduate School of Management at the Pitt Street lecture rooms. Up to a hundred and twenty people watched philosophy lecturer Robert Spillane and five other people debate the proposition "that H.R. is out of control."

Nobody needed to explain the meaning of the initials H.R., much as a generation or two earlier nobody needed to explain the meaning of the initials S.S. Entering the room, more than three quarters of us answered a poll to say that company human resources departments, with their armies of supposed facilitators, were out of control.

Now the rules of the debate forbid us from quoting what debaters said during the debate, or assuming they believed what they argued. Those rules didn't extend to my brief conversation afterwards with Spillane and my fellow alumnus, the recently retired Julian. Spillane lamented that younger people knew nothing of history. "I ask them, 'Who won the Second World War: Churchill, Stalin, or Hitler?' They don't know who won the First World War. They're not even sure there was a Second World War."

(I repeated Spillane's words later that night to my fourteen-year-old eldest son. "Hitler must have lost, because he was dead," he replied. "Churchill?" I needed to tell him Stalin also won; communist dictators aren't talked about in school as much as fascist dictators are. Three years later, my son came seventh in the state in modern history.)

"Most of my work nowadays is with government departments," said Spillane. "They call me up, because no one under the age of thirty-five can write a report. They can't critically analyse anything."

"That's the generation," I suggested, "that learnt their public speaking in multicultural speaking competitions?"

"Exactly." Whole generations now come of age without an original thought.

We imagine our forebears living like sheep with their duties to

God and Country, but they could think and question. "Like Abraham Lincoln," said General Douglas MacArthur in April 1944, "I am a firm believer in the people and, if given the truth, they can be depended upon to meet any national crises. The great point is to bring before them the real facts."

In spite of our humanist claims otherwise, the West no longer believes in the people, not our people. Authorities don't bring before people real facts, not about race and culture. We fear the repercussions.

"*Learn from yesterday, live for today, hope for tomorrow*," wrote Jewish scientist Albert Einstein in *Relativity: The Special and the General Theory*, published in 1916. A century later, we live for today all right, but we don't learn from yesterday and don't think much about tomorrow. "The important thing is to not stop questioning," he said. We stopped questioning.

"When the facts change, I change my mind," said British economist John Maynard Keynes. "What do you do?" Keynes died in 1946. Since then, if not already, that approach fell out of favour.

Our forebears were never as moronic as we are with multiculturalism; we know nothing else. We need to believe certain fundamental tenets about different races living together: that it's necessary, and it's desirable. Our rejection of judgement is a rejection of not just critical analysis, but any analysis. We prefer a poetic philosophy for a single human species in harmony, but without the questioning once intrinsic to Western philosophies. Multiculturalism depends upon it.

The first Friday in June 2013, my wife and I attended the morning assembly at our local primary school to see our youngest daughter receive her banner and second son his medal. The class item by one of the school's youngest classes involved boys and girls dressed in the colours and styles of the Aboriginal flag, reciting lovely things about Aborigines they'd almost certainly never encountered, beyond the cultural troupes coming periodically to perform.

As a prelude to the finals of the multicultural speaking competition following the assembly, the acting school principal spoke of all people being the same. She went onto say the thirty-two percent of children in the school from non-English speaking backgrounds (that was to say, other races) enriched us. Only four days later, lying alone in bed, did I wonder how they enriched us if we're all the same? I'd learnt to stop thinking in primary school assemblies; that's part of the purpose behind Harmony Day. We'd learnt to stop thinking altogether.

Education became inculcation very well done, with tireless repetition never seeming repetitive. In the choice between knowledge and ideology, we teach ideology. We call it knowledge.

We're not feeding facts but decrees. Education is based no longer upon facts but upon what educators call themes, the most pervasive of which are about people. The slogans of Harmony Day are beautiful themes to be sure: love, peace, and unity. The simpler they are, the more we like slogans, but they shut out our chance to learn.

Facts aren't the focus of Harmony Day. Harmony is. At best, themes make facts superfluous: thematic postmodernism. At worst, themes make them dangerous. Facts might lead us to question the themes we've been taught. Ideas might come to mind.

In my last years of school, I referred in a general studies essay to the complications Canada experienced with more than one official language. Never acknowledging the elitism of his opinions, my teacher criticised my view as elitist. In a world of multiple languages, we had to accommodate them at home.

I asked my modern history teacher if we should cater our final Higher School Certificate examination answers to the probable political opinions of the markers. A classmate Scott L muttered, "Stupid question."

He was right, but not for the reason he thought. Of course, we should cater to those opinions. Anything else would cost us marks. Our lives and careers depend upon us conforming to powerful people's opinions; we dare not question what they say. Education was becoming a matter of compliance.

In her final year of school, my second daughter's year had two classes the morning of Multicultural Day. In an education system where not much was compulsory, a teacher told the students they couldn't leave the school after their classes. "Multicultural Day is compulsory and it's fun," she insisted. To prevent students escaping, teachers locked the school gates and patrolled the area in cars.

Our children can't hide. Rachel's mother excused her from the multicultural speaking competition at our children's primary school because of the political indoctrination and complexities of the topics imposed upon year-four children, which necessitated parents preparing their speeches with them. Teachers rarely contacted parents, but the teacher the children called Mrs Lounge contacted Rachel's mother. The school compelled Rachel to participate.

My wife suggested our second son choose a comparatively innocuous topic about the Australian flag. He spoke of the flag's history and competitions to choose it, without daring to mention the British connections our founding fathers intended.

An education system predicated upon critical analysis would ask questions instead of dictating answers, challenge children to be specific with their platitudes, and judge students by their logic and reasoning instead of their points of view. What successes can multiculturalism boast that racial homogeneity can't? Why are governments, the police, media, and we to blame because some races fare poorly, decade after decade? Is racial diversity good? Is racism bad? Is multiculturalism worthwhile? Why must we try?

With ideologies down pat, we're not so good with ideas. Believing so much we've been told, we're not trying to learn because we think we already know. We depend upon what we've heard and read, but the little we know needn't affect what we fervently believe. We're trusting, certain of the sincerity of strangers. We don't know enough to question.

Addressing another rare assembly I attended at our local primary school, the headmistress (the third during my children's time there) said the planet Mars would come so close to the Earth later that month as to appear the size of the moon. Children, parents, and teachers dutifully believed her, while I whispered to my wife beside me, "It's not true."

Afterwards, I approached the headmistress. Quietly, I told her, "It's not true."

"I heard it on the radio."

"It's a hoax," I assured her.

Her mistake didn't embarrass her, if indeed she believed me instead of the radio. Errors in fact aren't errors anymore.

In 2012, the American state of Tennessee tried to reintroduce critical analysis to public education. Bill HB0368 required schools to *"Create an environment within public elementary and secondary schools that encourages students to explore scientific questions, learn about scientific evidence, develop critical thinking skills, and respond appropriately and respectfully to differences of opinion about controversial issues."* There was uproar because schools could no longer prohibit teachers "*from helping students understand, analyse, critique, and review in an objective manner the scientific strengths and scientific weaknesses of existing scientific theories covered in the course being taught, such as evolution and global warming.*"

The examples could as easily have included issues of race and culture among our rigid doctrinal demands. Western children don't grow up rejecting dissident viewpoints. They grow up unaware dissident viewpoints exist.

Schools outside the West mightn't critically analyse anything, but they're promoting themselves and their cultures, not denigrating them. If there's harmony, then racial homogeneity allows it. They don't need Harmony Day.

Neither did my school, during my racially almost-homogenous childhood. Rather than rules demanding we celebrate diversity around my classroom walls, we had multiplication tables, as none of my children's classrooms did. We learnt little things like reading, writing, and arithmetic.

Being taught endlessly about racial harmony and white people's racism leaves children less time to learn facts and logic. In 2012, the Australian Council for Educational Research reported the results of a national survey of students in school years six and ten, conducted late the previous year. Three quarters of year-six students and forty percent of year-ten students thought cotton came from animals. More than a quarter of year-six students and thirteen percent of year-ten students thought yoghurt grew on trees.

What happens in schools happens in universities. Sheltered at the McMahon Street wharf waiting for the mining industry cruise on Sydney Harbour, the cold and wet second Friday of July 2010, were two chemical engineers from Sydney University. The East Asian had little to say, each of us nibbling Grain Wave chips I'd never before seen. Much older than I was, the other man was close enough, he said, to see "the horizon of his working life." He said "every single" historian at the university was a Marxist. "Wouldn't you like to have just one person on your faculty that isn't a Marxist, just to have a different perspective?" he'd asked one.

The Marxist replied, "No!"

Schools, universities, and workplaces across communist Eastern Europe had political officers and compulsory studies of Marxism. Ours have become no less doctrinaire, as increasingly are our infant preschools and childcare. They prepare us for adulthoods in denial of the reality of multiculturalism: the decline of our countries, cities, and communities.

Agreeing with our multicultural wonder is much easier than thinking or challenging anyone about it; we're busy enough as it is. Our jobs, families, and football teams don't leave us time to examine the orthodoxies around us. We're sheep because being sheep is simpler than being shepherds, or defying the sheepdogs barking.

For all our talk of diversity, we have none of ideas and opinion, no intellectual plurality, not about anything important. What we call the intelligentsia is more a matter of profession and opinionated self-certainty than intelligence, relegating genii to the idiot masses if their politics veer from the norm: ideology supplanting intellect. Other ideas might be right, even brilliant, but nobody listens and nobody learns.

Few things threaten the unthinking more than a thought. Nothing threatens the unthinking more than a thought uttered aloud, particularly one uttered without conviction that it be true or false by a person thinking about it. Any twit can condemn a thought, some wisdom allows a person to rebuke it, but the greatest wisdom is required of the person who considers what's credible, whatever the outcome of that consideration. Errors can be as useful as accuracies in learning the truth.

Scholars deliberate upon propositions right or wrong, in the spirit with which they are made. Good ideas need air to germinate. Bad ideas need conversation to wither. I've learnt as much from people with whom I disagree as from those with whom I agree.

People who insist something is true because it is true, whatever the illogic and lack of evidence, don't suffer being challenged. The foolish restrict debate more than the wise. The wrong more than the right fear the truth.

If I were content for life to be a debate, I'd be content to contribute in some small way to debate. I'm not so content; I have too many children for that. Having just one child might've made talk inadequate.

The problem with critical analysis is that we end up with books like mine. This book isn't only about Western countries since we allowed interracial immigration, but about the extraordinary and exacting measures we're taking to console and cajole each other through. We can learn much from the world away from fictions portrayed in novels and textbooks, and on television and cinema screens, however lovely those fictions are. I describe a world many of us don't recognise, but if my writing seems a little (or more) biased one way, then it's because so much other writing, broadcasting, and entertainment is biased the other.

I write for anyone willing to wonder and learn; I wonder more than I know. I don't seek to cater to people already agreeing with me or to wage war against people who don't, leaving others disinterested or bemused. They can all sit with me drinking hot chocolate, rosehip infusion, wine, or cold beer, talking of what we know or suppose. I'd be pleased to keep learning more from what I read and hear than from what I write and say; the people I've met and events I've experienced taught me most that I know.

My qualifications to write are no more or less than those of any other able-bodied person. They're those of a deaf man trying to listen, blind woman trying to see, or fool trying to think. I write without ideology, idealism, or simply believing the advertisements, marketing, and spin, but venture forth ideas with all the sense and nonsense they speak for themselves. I'd rather be the only person who's right, than be wrong with everyone else.

I don't write to win debates, but to facilitate them. What matters isn't whether people agree beforehand, but whether they agree afterwards. Debates don't end by being avoided.

5. THE END OF SOCIETY

As part of the Diverse Australia Programme, the Australian government for Harmony Day 2010 issued children with colourful, little, round, metal badges bearing the caption *"Everyone Belongs."* We believe what we read on badges.

"On Harmony Day, let's…," began cards in sealed plastic pouches enclosing the badges, *"Honour our tradition of a fair go."* We've redefined our traditions into multiculturalism our forebears never imagined. *"Appreciate the benefits of cultural diversity."* We don't think of the costs. *"Respect each other."* We needn't respect our own. *"Mark the day with a celebration of our successes as a vibrant, cohesive, inclusive nation and wear this badge, along with your fellow Australians to show that EVERYONE BELONGS."* We consider our nations vibrant, cohesive, and inclusive, without imagining what they'd be had they remained homogeneous. We believe in Harmony Day.

With our family video camera, I attended the assembly at our children's primary school the Friday before Harmony Day, 2011 to see my youngest daughter perform in her class item. She and our second son received merit awards. It was probably the only time I filmed the headmistress addressing a school assembly, but I was working on this book and she talked about Harmony Day. Much of her speech she read, and I wondered if the words were hers or from the Department of Education. She explained (as if her audience had never before heard) that the purpose of Harmony Day was to show that the school welcomed everyone, that Australia was a place where everyone belonged.

In a rare diversion from what she read, she spoke of the recent school Welcome Night one Saturday evening, which three hundred people attended, demonstrating the school was a community. Yet, it had been no less striking that night than it had been at any other social night at our children's schools how few, if any, of the faces attending weren't white. Our societies that survived small numbers of other races haven't survived large enough numbers for them to become their own communities.

Many years earlier, before the introduction of Harmony Day, one of the first courses for my Master of Business Administration degree was in strategic behaviour. The lecturer grouped students into teams of eight members by our surnames. My surname, adjoining Lee, placed me among several Chinese. Among them was Swan, married with two young children, whose employer, the New South Wales government, gave him two hours a week study time in addition to whatever else he required. No employer was more generous.

The group charged members with particular tasks sharing the workload. Swan researched matters for our project, but I discovered by chance that he withheld most of his research from the rest of the group in a secret stash so only he could use it in the final exam. We worked together, but weren't a team. We weren't friends, as I understood friends to be.

At the beginning of the following term, when Swan knew how well or poorly the rest of us had done in our first term courses, Swan knew I'd done well. That made working with me in his interest. He became the only person whose invitation to join a group I ever refused.

Russia's President Dmitry Medvedev drew from his pocket a sample coin, minted in Belgium, at the meeting of heads of the Group of Eight leading industrial nations in L'Aquila, Italy in July 2009. Like the European Euro, currency would be a means to our new Western vision of a single seamless world, replacing the American dollar as the world's de facto reserve currency when America's financial crisis was destabilising its worth. Whereas America's currency said "*In God We Trust*," our defining words are "*Unity in Diversity*."

Never have I seen unity in diversity, beyond the most particular tasks at hand. The only cohesive communities and workforces I've experienced were racially and religiously homogenous; perhaps I've been lucky, or unlucky. Society requires commonality about something. Diversity leaves people disparate and divided. Our governments, educators, and scriptwriters have tried very hard to dictate our values and often succeeded, but they haven't created commonality either based upon diversity or in spite of it. Racial harmony means races leaving each other alone, not getting in each other's way.

In 2011, I was surprised to discover that the District Court's

Equal Opportunities Tribunal in South Australia allowed British defence company BAE Systems to refuse to employ Sudanese, Chinese, and Vietnamese. "In the defence industry space there are exemptions…," explained defence minister Stephen Smith, "provided the legal processes and the appropriate processes are gone through…"

Presuming there were no physical, mental, or psychological issues in play, we must have recognised the racial and religious loyalties people of other races retain. It begged the suggestion that if military interests justified racial discrimination, so might other national, social, familial, and personal interests.

Katoomba exudes much of old Australia, with the booths in the Paragon Café and antique stores nearby. The Blue Mountains City Council banners hanging from the light poles along Katoomba Street, in the winter of 2011, decreed new Australia. "*Many Peoples, One Community, Many Cultures,*" in an Aboriginal flag might have referred to Aboriginal peoples or to all of us defined by their Aboriginality: multiracialism in the framework of Aboriginal peoples and culture. Mixing "*Diversity, Unity, Strength,*" in other banners was ridiculous.

Many peoples and cultures Australia might geographically have become, but we aren't one community. We have no unity. Strength is just a word. A few generations earlier, when the Blue Mountains were so cherished a holiday place, there'd been community, unity, and strength. We didn't need banners telling us so. If there were flags, then they were our flags: Australia and Britain.

Topics for the 2012 multicultural speaking competition at our local primary school included the idea of being part of a group, but not race, country, or religion beyond a neighbourhood church. The rare reference to family and even rarer reference to church might've been the result of the class discussion that preceded the competition, as might the other groups mentioned: sport, creative arts, clubs, school, and friends. Marking them with uniforms supposedly offered members belonging and that most important of traits to the postmodern West, equality, but none of the groups reached very far or meant very much.

Without community, there are only moments of coincident individual interests we call networks. Purushottam Chhatre was a manufacturing leader at Mondelez International with two hundred and thirty-four connections to his Linked In computer site profile,

THE FAILURE OF MULTICULTURALISM

but who didn't stop after his car killed a pedestrian in a suburban street at Forest Hill, Melbourne in August 2013.

In three of the four collisions between moving vehicles in which I have been involved, the other driver and I stopped our cars, exchanged details, and did everything properly. In each of those three cases, the other driver was also Australian. It was civil society, but society was fading. Sydney was becoming multicultural.

In the fourth case, in September 2007, the other driver was Korean: Allen Kim. The collision was his fault: speeding, illegally crossing double unbroken lines, and crashing into the driver side of my turning car in front of me. I was half a metre from being killed.

Three of my children with me in my car could also have been killed, especially my youngest son sitting behind me. He was crying. My middle son's forehead was gashed, blood sprayed. My eldest daughter felt internal pain from her seatbelt.

Allen Kim tried to drive quickly away, but could not. Carrying a mobile telephone, he called for a single tow truck, for him. He also summoned his friends.

He did not approach our wrecked car. We depended upon people hearing the crash coming from their homes and passers by calling for an ambulance and the police.

When the police arrived, Allen Kim bounced up to a policeman. His only interest was in lying: that his car had broken down up the hill. The woman who had been in the car behind him was there to tell the police he lied, but still Kim persisted with his lie.

A policeman needed to dress Allen Kim down twice for laughing so much with his friends about the collision. With several driving offences already accrued, he would lose his licence.

A student at a prestigious private school he named, Allen Kim and his parents in their new Waitara apartment refused to pay the costs of replacing my car. When I told him I would sue him, aged eighteen, he became irate. Insisting he had examinations for which he needed to study, he insisted I leave him be. Neither Kim nor his family asked after my children.

People to whom I told the story without mentioning Kim's name naughtily guessed he was Asian. Allen Kim was Korean, as were his friends.

Our part-Maori friend had hosted scores of Korean, Chinese, and Japanese students in her home. "They're all arrogant," she whispered, where no one else could hear her, "except the

Japanese." All the people who helped my family and me were Australian.

Allen Kim did not care if we thought poorly of him. We care. We make excuses he did not.

We say rightly that white people often no longer paid damages incurred by them or their children to others, but in our time of racial homogeneity we were a society. Being a society, we felt moral obligations. We had become individuals.

We'd say we cause motor vehicle collisions too, unconcerned we did not cause that one, unless the collision was my fault for being on the road that afternoon impeding Kim's journey. It might have been the fault of the woman driving her car behind mine because her car obstructed Kim's view of my indicator lights before he crossed the unbroken lines. Perhaps she and I should have apologised to Kim, giving him money in recompense.

We exhort diversity, thrilled that Allen Kim and his parents came to Australia. We'd be no less thrilled if he had killed my children and me.

6. THE END OF AUTHORITY

We'd have rarely accepted instructions from other races before World War II. Our increasing enthusiasm for doing so since then has made other races less willing than ever to take instructions from us. At the New South Wales railways during the 1990s, my wife's cousin Stuart managed a workforce principally comprising Lebanese, who by and large refused to take his instructions. Whether that was because they were Lebanese or because he wasn't, I don't know.

Western multiculturalism and individualism are never more obviously intertwined than in the end of any sense of authority, structure, or society. Social structures arise with the force not of law but tribalism, which we've dismissed. Like people from other races, we individuals only respect Western authority when doing so is in our individual interests.

The rules of our local primary school demanded respect for other races, not ours. "I don't have to listen to you," a year-one boy told my wife when she came to teach Scripture to his class. "You're not important."

Another child explained why teachers like my wife weren't important. "You don't give awards."

Kathryn came to teach my second son's composite years-four and five class about craft. (Composite classes epitomise our pursuit of equality, not just among pupils but among teachers.) A few of the boys told her to "F*** off!"

Boys and girls played the system not of education but awards, saying what they needed to say. However obnoxious they were to everyone else, they fawned to the teachers that mattered. Daijing was awarded Aussie of the Month expressly for "having a lovely smile," which I gather from my wife was among the ugliest smiles around. She must have offered it often enough to someone important.

The awards were good preparation for life. Those same awful children would become awful adults, and be awarded Australian of the Year. (The only qualification the hitherto-unknown David Morrison appeared to have to be 2016 Australian of the Year was the force with which he condemned white Australia for the racism that supposedly held other races back and for prejudice against Muslims. At least he was Australian.)

What struck me from their names and photographs in the school newsletters were that Aussies of the Month were disproportionately from other countries, even those only in Australia for a time before headed home again. The purpose of the award wasn't to reward any kind of excellence or achievement, but to tell us those children were Australian. Their citizenship, residency, and senses of identity were immaterial. They might never have called themselves Aussie, but that didn't matter to us. We weren't trying to change them. We were trying to change us.

Expressing our vision of ourselves as well as ever, Paula was awarded Aussie of the Month in August 2013 without even pretending to be Australian. "*She has overcome language barriers and cultural differences to blend into the Australian way of life but still keeping the values and culture of her home country.*" Multicultural harmony means immigrants keep their home country's values and culture. The Australian way of life is something other than values and culture: perhaps nothing more than wearing a hat in the sun. Little wonder the West became superficial.

It's hard to imagine Ali Farhat cared about Aussie of the Month in a mathematics class at Ashfield Boys' High School the last Friday of July 2001. After teacher Helen Alkan confronted two boys passing an item between them, he produced what seemed a real gun, pointed it towards her, and pulled the trigger up to eight times. "Die bitch, die," he yelled.

Only because she wasn't shot did Alkan realise the gun was a toy. Farhat was suspended from school for ten days, but never charged over the incident. Alkan was away for nine weeks. "I was consistently scared if he was going to come into the room," she said of her return to work on light duties. "I was scared of other kids." The noise of a student slamming a book on a table or a car backfiring made her jump. "I kept seeing his face. I would look at my dad or my brother, and I kept seeing his face and the gun."

The incident led to Alkan retiring five years later on medical grounds. Nine years later, she still suffered depression, anxiety, and post-traumatic stress disorder and was often admitted to hospital.

The only reason her story reached a newspaper I read was because she'd initiated court action, but not against Farhat, his family, or the Australian Department of Immigration and Citizenship. Her suit was against the New South Wales Department of Education for not having warned her of the boy's history of violence and for letting him stay at the school. She clearly didn't understand the need to celebrate diversity.

The day after Harmony Day 2011, a fourteen-year-old pupil at Nightcliff Middle School in Darwin punched his relief teacher before stabbing him with a knife. Northern Territory education minister Chris Burns didn't just trivialise the assault. He saw the positive aspect. "I commend our teachers for the difficulties they encounter with behaviour...," he said, "they deal with them well." He thought four assaults by students against teachers in 2010, out of thirty-three thousand students in the Northern Territory school system, was rather few.

We don't punish wrongdoers. We support them. "This student has received support for behavioural problems in the past," said Burns, noting that volatile behaviour among children was often the result of events outside the classroom or school.

When I was young, teachers reprimanding students could expect support from the students' parents. Nowadays, many parents add to the problem.

Following his child's poor performance in the selective schools entrance examination, Doctor Rajaratnam Premachandran complained about Jennie Ryan, principal of Beecroft Public School, to the Department of Education. He also wrote to her, calling her racist and possibly a physical danger to his children. *"You will suffer for the rest of your life for such nasty and dirty behaviour,"* he told her. Distributing his electronic messages to a growing audience including the Indian High Commissioner, he described her as *"incompetent, dishonest and untrustworthy,"* demanding she resign. In 2009, she sued him for defamation.

"Indian doctors," sighed my wife (presuming he was a doctor of medicine), as we watched the television news. When she'd taught at a prestigious private girls' school, an Indian doctor complained so much about everyone, the headmistress invited him to bring his list of complaints to the school at the start of each term to make them easier to answer. To compound the annoyance, if anything could, that doctor was the father of triplets.

That doctor also made an impact outside the school, reaching the newspapers. Many years earlier, he'd sought Liberal Party selection in a nearby electorate. Alleging fraud in the vote, he demanded ballot papers be counted again. By the passion of his complaints, a casual reader might have thought he'd almost succeeded, but of the hundred or so votes, he'd received only one.

Our schools are dangerous places not just for teachers, but also for people nearby. Paramedic Karen Matthews was treating a patient injured in a car crash outside Berala Public School just after three o'clock the first Monday afternoon of March 2011, when Ali Mobayad double parked in a school zone. Out of his car, he pounded her Rapid Response vehicle's driver-side window and began yelling and swearing at the ambulance officer. Her fear of physical violence prevented her from tending to her patient.

Attending Burwood Local Court the last day of that month, Mobayad saw a waiting journalist and camera. "You see this face," he said angrily, "if you use that image you will never see the end of this. I don't care what happens to me, I'll kill you if you use that photo...you f***ing idiot!"

The *Daily Telegraph* newspaper published the photograph. It didn't name the journalist or photographer.

Rugby league coach Roy Masters stepped deftly around our taboos about race in his 2009 newspaper article, 'Big issue no one is game to tackle.' From him, I learnt that forty percent of players in the National Rugby League competition were what he called "*Pacific Island origin*," as were more than half the young players. The fear of being accused of racism, wrote Masters, meant no one else mentioned it. His article was meticulously careful to avoid saying anything negative about Islanders, while revealing that Australians were wary of playing a sport where huge Islanders trampled upon them.

Sydney Samoan Council representative Richard David acknowledged that Pacific Islanders and Lebanese were responsible for increased violence at rugby league matches, as referees had claimed, but blamed the referees. "When they walk out on to the pitch some of them don't realise that comments they make to the players could be hurtful to them," he said. "They also don't realise some of the Islander boys don't have respect for them from kick-off and that sometimes manifests in violence." (We needed to be culturally sensitive to that fact that other races don't respect us.) "I think it's unfair to pinpoint the Pacific Islander community, but I admit there is a problem when it comes to communication." David blamed violence on a lack of dialogue.

When we acknowledge problems between races, we too imagine they can be overcome with a chat. Barry Taylor, a friend of mine in the Liberal Party, was among those agreeing with political candidate Mark Majewski that we just needed to get the divided races of Western Sydney talking to each other.

The night after I read Richard David's words, I was at our local scout hall. Another man named David was talking about his schoolboy son playing rugby union, several times dislocating his shoulder and once breaking it. He mentioned the Islanders, to which I repeated the suggestion that the problem was a failure of communication.

"It's not," he said. "They don't respect authority." Europeans could never referee games involving Islanders and Lebanese. "They're different."

"We're not allowed to say that," I told him.

"It's true," he said, as if that entered into it. "When they make a mistake," he said of the Islanders, "when they knock the ball on, they get angry."

I recalled his words early the next morning, lying safely in my bed. When I'd visited Western Samoa and the Cook Islands twenty-three years earlier, the Islanders respected the authority of their own.

When I studied at law school, jurisprudence was a compulsory subject, from which we chose one of six streams. I selected international and comparative jurisprudence, as I studied all the international law I could. The course focused upon the Garia and other tribes of Papua New Guinea, which Peter Lawrence had visited, studied, and about whom he'd written a book. Lawlessness in cities like Port Moresby, which condemned Western expatriates to living in barbed-wired compounds, was due to Melanesians living away from their families and clans. They were rascals.

Tribespeople don't defer to authorities outside their tribes, not even others of their race. That's not to say there are no crimes within communities and families, but people who would've been peaceful in their tribally homogenous villages become violent in other environments. Pacific Islanders, Arabs, Africans, and Native Americans remain tribal without structured societies outside of their tribes. Perhaps we all do. For much of Asia, people's tribes are their race.

When rioting broke out in a housing estate at Rosemeadow, Sydney in January 2009, acting premier Carmel Tebbutt spoke of the need to build social cohesion. Residents told police and other outsiders to keep away from their suburb.

I assumed the rioters were Australian, given the images of Rosemeadow on the evening news were of white-skinned men, women, and children. Among the people appearing before court, the only one whose image I saw published appeared white. No news report mentioned anyone's race, even when police pleaded with elders to help control their people. It would be nice to think of white people taking heed of our elders, or even acknowledging we have elders, but we don't. When the elders of Rosemeadow called for calm and a curfew, their races became visible. They were Aborigines and an Islander.

The only authorities are within tribes and races. After six Africans raped a fourteen-year-old Islander girl for more than half an hour in Bill Colbourne Reserve, Blacktown in February 2014, Father Chris Riley (from Youth off the Streets) deployed strike force teams of African social workers to act like a police force. They'd rush to incidents of racial tension between Africans and Islanders or sexual assault in Blacktown and Doonside within five to ten minutes.

Sudanese lawyer Deng Thiak Adut blamed the tensions not on the rapists, but on the police. They'd described the rapists they were trying to find as being of "African appearance."

None of the news reports I'd read mentioned the rapists' race. One indiscriminate radio report I'd heard mentioned them being African. "Will there be any racial violence?" asked Adut. "I would say 'yes' because of what is being reported."

True to the spirit of Harmony Day, we don't imagine crime causing racial tensions. We only imagine mentioning a criminal's race causing tensions.

Police are little more effective than other authorities across racial and tribal lines. In 2013, the New South Wales government responded to the victims of shootings around Sydney refusing to speak with police by watering down our traditional rights to silence. Judges and juries could thus draw inferences from suspects being silent they couldn't previously draw. The rights and liberties that functioned in British Australia weren't functioning among Arabs.

Policing adds to our problems. Black people feel police are prejudiced against them whenever the suspects police seek are black. Muslims feel motivated to become terrorists by police operations apprehending Muslim terrorists. They all expect Western police to leave them alone. Multiculturalism means we can't leave each other alone.

In 2015, the Australian Federal Police invited Muslims to feasts in Sydney and Melbourne to celebrate the end of Ramadan. Eight hundred and fifty Muslims urged their leaders to boycott the dinners for trying "*to create a false image of cooperation, harmony and trust which could not be further from the truth.*" The Sydney dinner was cancelled, which the Concerned Muslims Australia group called proof of the "*abundant strength in the unity of the Muslim community.*"

Our multicultural vision presumes justice is objective. It's not. Without commonality, one person's justice is another tribe's or race's injustice. Justice is subjective.

7. TRIBAL CONFLICT

During my Business studies, a lecturer showed a short film portraying a Filipina woman in an Australian workplace. Afterwards, the hundred or more students discussed means by which the Australians should support her.

Not me. "She was pretty abusive about Australians," I pointed out.

The audience, or at least the Australians, groaned. Some roared. In response to the Filipina's abuse, theirs had been a graceful silence, but there was no grace or silence to me. When the ruckus abated, speakers resumed suggesting what Australians should do.

"Everyone noticed it," my friend Phil said to me afterwards, of the Filipina's abuse, "but you were the only one who mentioned it."

Rather than being so rude or racist as to mention other races' rudeness, we accept their improprieties. I never mentioned them again.

Multiculturalism depends upon individualism: people not becoming involved when someone of their race or religion feels offended, mistreated, or hurt. Only white people buy into it.

After sixteen-year old Afghan immigrant Hussein Khavari raped and murdered nineteen-year-old German student Maria Ladenburger in Freiburg in October 2016, her parents asked well-wishers to donate money to a refugee charity. Her father was European Commission lawyer Clemens Ladenburger.

Other races retain their familial, tribal, and racial loyalties we rarely recognise. Defying someone from their race means defying their race, as we can no longer conceive.

Arian, who called himself Achmed, Ariel, and other names, was short, fat, and strong. Faraz was tall and beefy. Kiayan was more average in height, but also beefy. They were all Australian born and might've never seen Iran, but proudly called themselves, "T.P.C.s," meaning "Tough Persian C..."

Early in their first year of high school and without any clear reason, Arian and Faraz bailed my eldest son up in the school library. The only child among my son's school friends Arian didn't assault was David. "He has Persian blood in him," explained Arian.

If Faraz ever got wind of another student saying anything critical of his race, he bundled up to the child and ask, "Did you say s**t about Persians?"

Sensibly, the child denied it.

If Faraz didn't believe the child, he beat the child. Even if he did believe the child, he might beat the child.

Persians, like other races, didn't tease their own. They fought anyone of another race who did.

Not us. White boys at the school didn't bully boys of other races for fear of being taken aside for racism. They bullied other white boys. (Within a few years after finishing school, Arian was gaoled for drug trafficking.)

In 2015, America's Department of Education reported a School Crime Supplement to the National Crime Victimisation Survey using National Centre for Education Statistics. Twenty-four percent of white students aged twelve to eighteen had been bullied at school, but only twenty percent of blacks, nineteen percent of Hispanics, and nine percent of Asians. Students bullied were more likely to struggle in school, miss classes, abuse substances, and commit suicide.

More often than not, tribes and conflict are racial. The West responded to racial conflict by abandoning our race. Other races respond by affirming theirs. Hempstead High School, New York endured days of brawling between scores of black and Hispanic students in October 2008.

We worked hard to soothe racial divisions, while African refugees created criminal precincts across Minneapolis St Paul. On Valentine's Day 2013, the Minneapolis Public Schools chief of communications, Stan Alleyne, issued a statement saying Minneapolis South High was a school that continually made the district proud. "South is a very diverse high school," he said. "It is a microcosm of the city. Students function together at a high level every day. That is the strength of this school. Our students live diversity every day."

They were beautiful words typical of those we like to speak and hear. What made them so fascinating was that they weren't issued in response to academic excellence or anything else meritorious. They followed what Minneapolis police officer William Palmer called "a food fight that escalated into a physical fight" between Somalis and other Africans, which students from other races took the chance to join. Two to three hundred were involved. (Nothing is more likely to bring out accolades for our success with multiculturalism than immigrants attacking people.)

Students attributed the fight to long-simmering tensions between the eight percent of students who were Somali and the twenty percent who were other African. "I know it's a pride thing between Muslims and black people," said Symone Glasker. "They want their pride back for something, I don't know." She said "boys were hitting girls." Some lay on the floor with their hands over their heads, in surrender. "They didn't know if someone was going to bring out a knife, or if someone was going to bring out a gun." A school staff member was hit in the head with a bottle and taken to hospital.

Also hospitalised that day were three students with injuries unrelated to the fight. That was presumably a normal day at Minneapolis South High.

Metal fences in Soweto keep African tribes from killing each other. We blame white South African apartheid that ended decades ago, but African tribes have been killing each other since long before Europeans arrived. Black violence against white people contributed to the apartheid regime in the first place.

Julius Malema, the leader of the ruling African National Congress' youth league in 2011, stood before South African rallies singing a Zulu song exhorting Africans to "Awudubele (i)bhulu," or "shoot the Boer" or "shoot the farmer," meaning white farmers. There'd been several racially charged murders on farms, with black and white victims.

Zulus are just as hostile to Indians. Indians are hostile to them. David (the head of the parents and citizens association at my eldest son's high school) told me that in Natal, companies could hire Indians or Zulus, but if a company hired both, then they would kill each other on the factory floor. When Zulus realised they were becoming the minority in a town, they slayed two and a half thousand Indians one weekend.

The West also suffers home-grown homicide, but white criminals normally act alone. We're individuals.

Social breakdown necessitates the growth of gangs. They have the same disinterest for people outside their gangs that races have for other races and individuals have for everyone.

Sydney newspapers widely reported five teenagers armed with a machete, samurai sword, and two baseball bats storming Merrylands High School in April 2008, assaulting two female students and two teachers. Police reports mentioned they were boys and their ages. One early news report, tucked away near the end, mentioned they were all Pacific Islanders. Long reports of prosecutions and appeals for leniency from the courts never mentioned race again.

Three years later, the *Daily Telegraph* newspaper revealed the Islanders had possibly been members of the Gee-40 gang. The first Thursday in February 2011, up to a hundred young people armed with baseball bats and crude homemade weapons brawled outside the Westfield Centre, Mount Druitt. Scores of New South Wales police and specialist officers from the riot and dog squads, supported by helicopters, intervened, arresting thirteen. Race was relevant to news reports because the brawl was between Islander gangs: the Gee-40 and Mounty County. Thus the rest of us need not feel alarmed.

We even found a chance to say good things about Islanders. "Police were aware of some intelligence, thankfully," said police officer McMahon, "that came to us from very good work from specialist units and members of the Pacific Islander community that are law abiding, and because of that we were able to marshal considerable numbers of specialist police here." (Those Islanders alerted the police to protect their people from each other.)

Human nature is to defend tribes and families, but not us. We thus taper our dealings with other races.

New South Wales police from the Middle Eastern Crime Squad were reluctant to raid homes in Sydney suburban Auburn in November 2009 for fear of generating another riot. (Critics have complained about the New South Wales police operating Middle Eastern and Asian crime squads making those immigrants feel unwelcome, but they're not named for the races of victims.) Rumbling tensions between rival crime groups could again break into a gun battle as it had done in March that year, with bullets hitting several homes.

While we tell our children that other children being naughty is no excuse for them being naughty, gang membership can alleviate punishments for other races. Accounting student Kanan

Kharbanda was walking his friend to Sunshine railway station in 2008 when they came across a group of Africans, including eighteen-year-old Sudanese refugee Majang Ngor. One African demanded a dollar, before hitting Kharbanda in the face. The other Africans joined in, kicking and punching Kharbanda, hitting and kicking his friend to the ground. Kharbanda suffered a broken nose and fractured eye socket. He lost the sight in his right eye.

Two years later, Judge Susan Cohen excused Ngor from a gaol sentence for the attack because she believed at least three other Africans, too young to be named, were more culpable than he was. The Children's Court had only subjected them to youth supervision orders for nine months. Besides, Ngor had finished school, obtained a stable job, and stopped binge-drinking alcohol, apparently to his credit. Convinced the public benefit lay with his rehabilitation, she ordered him to perform forty hours of community work (without specifying which community).

Court cases reveal all sorts of interesting things. Suing the New South Wales Department of Education in 2008 for allegedly breaching its duty of care towards him, an Australian Lebanese claimed that he suffered Asian phobia. Never before had I read of someone from a race other than ours supposedly suffering such a phobia, but we weren't trying to silence him. He was a plaintiff pleading a case for compensation.

He'd been in year eleven at Birrong Boys High School, with what his legal counsel called "deeply entrenched racial divisions" between Lebanese, Australian, Asian, and Tongan students. A misunderstanding with a Vietnamese boy led to a scuffle that two teachers broke up. The Vietnamese and three other Asian boys later bashed him, knocked him to the ground, kicked him, and stabbed him, before a teacher again intervened. He suffered a collapsed left lung, puncture wounds, and abrasions.

After his release from hospital and return to school, fellow students warned him, "The Asians were coming to finish the job." Complaining to the school principal, he saw through the principal's office window a group of Asians gathering across the road. The principal drove him home. He never returned to the school. Psychiatric treatment didn't keep him from still suffering entrenched stress ten years later, compelling him to flee to Dubai where Asian men were few.

Criminal gangs are the most violent expression of people's tribal natures. Only white people don't associate them with race.

It took a battle between up to twenty Asian men and three doormen in Chinatown, Sydney, around midnight the last Saturday in May 2010 to reveal the existence of the CCB: the Chinese City Boys. A criminal gang in the style of Chinese triads, they returned to Mr B's Hotel at three thirty that Sunday morning and used a metal crowd-control post to smash a front window. The doormen were moved to other premises to protect them from retribution.

The Chinese City Boys shared Chinatown with traditional triad-based crime gangs 14K, Big Circle, and Sing Wa, none of which I imagined being mentioned in a multicultural speaking competition. More a model for multiculturalism was the 180 White Tigers gang, from which the Chinese City Boys came. Journalist Les Kennedy delightfully quoted it being called a "*rainbow*" gang for including "*youths with Asian, Caucasian, and Pacific Islander backgrounds*," although apparently not others.

It's hard to envisage gang members being so coy. The Chinese City Boys weren't the City Boys of Chinese Background. Chinatown wasn't the Town of Chinese Background.

In 2011, the *Daily Telegraph* newspaper described the gangs hanging around Sydney street corners, shopping malls, and train stations robbing children as young as ten years old and bashing teenagers, as well as scouring the suburbs for parties to ruin, as "*Australian thugs*," but their names included FBI. When I grew up, the acronym for the Federal Bureau of Investigations denoted heroic white Americans apprehending relatively innocuous white criminals, but these were Full Blooded Islanders. (We no longer think of people being full-blooded anything.)

Former assistant police commissioner Clive Small believed Sydney was home to more than two hundred street gangs. Deputy police commissioner Nick Kaldas was most concerned about the Muslim Brotherhood Movement, which "attracts disenfranchised youth who can be drawn to more sophisticated criminal groups for the lifestyle, the element of belonging, money, and power they believe this brings." They weren't joining to be individuals.

Adding to the problem was the arrival of what journalist Mark Morri called "*new Australians*," although I couldn't imagine those Pacific Islanders and Somalis, Sudanese and other African calling themselves Australians. Morri's interest was the role not of race or culture, but of social networking computer sites like Facebook and

Twitter. There was thus some irony that the article included the usual invitation to readers to *"Join us over on Facebook | Twitter."*

That same year, I read of someone wanting Facebook shut down because of its use not by criminal gangs, but by white people disseminating information critical of other races. Ironically, we credited the freedom to spread information around social networking sites with empowering people to revolution from their dictatorships in North Africa and the Middle East.

Multiracial places are no places for individuals. They're worst for people brave enough to be heroes.

Luke Mitchell intervened to protect a man being assaulted by three Asian men outside the Spot Nightclub in Brunswick, Melbourne in 2009. Shortly afterwards, Mitchell and his four friends were at a nearby convenience store when a car pulled up and two Asians stepped out. They stabbed him five times and kicked him as he lay defenceless on the ground, killing him.

In one of the most ridiculous comments about the murder, Victorian premier John Brumby called it "un-Australian." The killers had already fled to Thailand.

In commentary following the *Herald Sun* news report of the killing, Chan of Brisbane blamed alcohol, although the report said nothing about alcohol. Ben H of the Dandenong wanted to attack the root causes of violence in society, as if Melbourne remained a society beyond Mitchell's heroics. Aussie expat in Singapore lauded that country's low crime rates and suggested Australia also adopt the death penalty for murder and severe punishments such as caning for lesser crimes. Sam 21 of Melbourne thought the attackers needed counselling to deal with their insecurities. (We imagine cushy rounds of counselling ending crime.)

Anonymity allowed Wal to break from the pack. *"White Australia policy doesn't look too bad now!!"*

Anonymity also emboldened Jeannie of the Dream. *"There seems to be a predominance of Asian youth gangs causing a lot of trouble in Melbourne........OH MY GOD I'M RACIST..........but somebody had to say it. Why doesn't the government approach the leaders of these communities & form an approach where leaders of this community, parents, police & government work together to stamp this UNACCEPTABLE BEHAVIOUR OUT!! Another approach is to stop these violent cultures ever settling in our once peaceful country. Now I'll sit back & wait for the abuse......but instead of abusing me how about YOU giving us some good ideas to ponder in order that our streets are once again safe for decent law-abiding citizens to walk!!!!"*

The most interesting comment came from Pete of Victoria. "*I'm oz asian and I'd never go to the cheaper night clubs simply because of all the asian gang activity. You can see the criminal types hanging out together with Thai women here. I'll bet these guys are Thai men here on tourist visas and involved with illegal prostitution.... I hope the Thai police will cooperate and extradite them... RIP Luke Mitchell. a true blue hero. Our thoughts are with his family.*" Pete clearly wasn't Thai.

8. THE FAILURE
OF MULTIRACIAL LIBERALISM

"Free institutions are next to impossible in a country made up of different nationalities," wrote liberal philosopher John Stuart Mill in 1859. *"Among people without fellow-feeling, especially if they read and speak different languages, the united public opinion, necessary to the working of representative government, cannot exist."*

The West averted that problem by governing with little recourse to public opinion; we dismiss it for being populism. That lack of fellow feeling makes freedom of speech, democracy, universal suffrage, an independent judiciary, and other cornerstones of liberalism incompatible with multiculturalism. It's the same lack of fellow feeling in Western individualism, but at least we find a common opinion to demand our individualism. The failure of multiculturalism is akin to the failure of individualism.

There is no end of papers critical of multiculturalism I discovered when writing these books. What became amazing wasn't so much that such literature exists, but that we ever imagined we could form a functioning multiracial society. Any thoughtful person asked to foreshadow the consequences of open immigration and racial integration in 1939 would've spoken of problems among those that have arisen, without contemplating our determination to try so hard and give up so much in pursuit of our multicultural ideal. It took two world wars and a holocaust to make us try.

My eldest daughters' high school suspends all classes for Multicultural Day each year. Preparing for Multicultural Day the first Friday in March 2010, my eldest daughter brought home a poster for the children to colour, promising *"classroom 'country' visits, guest speaker, dancers, soccer, concert, fabulous food!"* (I assumed the word "country" was in quotation marks because we don't believe in countries anymore.) *"See the world at..."* concluded the poster, in its final and largest type, but students saw only a thin, romantic slice of world: dance, sport, music, and food.

Our lives would be different if our cities complied with those experiences, tripping from room to room. The big, wide, narrow, little world doesn't understand.

I noticed my daughter's poster lying on a bookshelf as I read a *Daily Telegraph* newspaper article headed 'Kings Cross gang muscles in on Gold Coast and Melbourne drug trade' on my computer monitor. The Notorious motorcycle gang referred to Kings Cross, Sydney as "Little Arabia" for the Arabs controlling the crime there. "They have got links to every industry from the post office to the police force, from Bob's Guns to Ahmed's Butchery, you know?" said Wahlid. "You get a handbook where you learn how to make drugs, how to make guns, where to get, what areas are controlled by the gang, everything like that." I bet none of that appeared in a classroom on Multicultural Day, except perhaps Ahmed's Butchery.

The article provoked the usual flurry of racist responses that anonymity allows and the hatred of racists that doesn't require anonymity. Shane Farra of God's Country was far more concerned about white people's racism than guns, drugs, and other crime (or for that matter, grammar and spelling). "*wow,*" he wrote in reply to the racism, "*looks like the anti-ethnic band wagon has rolled into town, these so called gang members are born in australian hospitals and educated in australian schools and have been exposed to western culture all there life. SHAME AUSTRLAIA SHAME.*"

The only culture we blame for crime is our own. So does everyone else.

"*The gang is there to supply a need like a shop owner,*" wrote Chris of Sydney, a Syrian. "*The drug trade is their main income and it is thriving because people can't stop snorting, injecting or taking pills. You go to a club and most people are coked up or hav taken pills. They do not understand that people get killed and threatened to get that drug into the users hand and they are simply helping it thrive.*"

He was right, although there'd be no drug problem without drugs. There wouldn't be that pain and death.

He blamed democracy. "*Because of democracy, Obama was right when he said the war on drugs cannot be won. You try to form a gang in a 3rd world country like syria where I grew up and you will be shot dead by the cops. They have zero tolerance for everything. Western countries help gangs to expand.*" The Western culture to blame for other races' crimes is liberalism.

"*DO NOT BLAME THE RACE,*" wrote in emphatic capital letters Tony Soprano of New Jersey, presumably a devotee of the television programme *The Sopranos*, *"their race is what brought these groups together. But their race does not tell them to commit the crime."*

That comment came back to mind as I sat in my car that evening, headed home from a brief trip to the supermarket. His was the categorical rejection of racial traits that so characterises the postmodern West. Nevertheless, he recognised race and people congregating around it.

Human instinct mightn't be to harm people without reason. Some races are quick to find reason.

Through the extensive news reporting of the brutal, unprovoked murder of policeman Glenn McEnallay in Matraville, Sydney in 2002 by two car-thief brothers, I'd never learnt the killers' race until one was deported to Tonga. "He has spent a lot of his life in Australia," complained their father, refuting any suggestion that Tongans might be particularly criminal because "his behaviour was based on the Australian environment."

The Australian environment must have been particularly influential on that family. His brother Motekiai Taufahema had spent more than half his twenty-one years in Australia in prison when he was released in 2009. He wasn't deported because that would have disadvantaged his seven-year-old daughter, born since he went to prison for McEnallay's murder. Two other siblings were in gaol. A fifth had been shot dead by police during an armed hold-up at the Canley Heights Hotel.

Running amok in east Melbourne the first week of June 2010 was a gang of car thieves, who released at least twenty handbrakes including eight that weekend. The cars rolled into power poles, fences, and street signs. Closed circuit television recorded them using credit cards stolen from the vehicles at stores and supermarkets in Monash, revealing them to be East Asian.

Asian criminals reputedly blame Western rights for their crimes. They come from countries where criminals can be caned, gaoled, and executed into a West where they're given healthcare, legal services, food, clothing, and counselling. Criminals in the West enjoy more rights than law-abiding people enjoy elsewhere. Whatever Western culture happens to be, it includes a flurry of freedoms in which we bask, which free other races to be criminal. They say we're thus culpable for the crimes they commit.

(Not even Singapore's strict laws and punishments prevented rioting in the Little India neighbourhood, the second Sunday night in December 2013. A bus had hit and killed a Bangladeshi worker.)

Relaxed Western policing and parenting fail with other races. "Also," said Mohammed Abbas explaining the Stockholm race riots of May 2013, "in Sweden you cannot hit your children to discipline them, and this is a problem for foreign parents. The kids can feel they can cause whatever trouble they want, and the police don't even arrest any of them most of the time."

Koreans who feared a backlash after Cho Seung Hui murdered thirty-two students and teachers at Virginia Polytechnic Institute the middle Monday of April 2007 misunderstood the West. Some responses were anti-Korean, but the prevailing Western attitude mirrored the view of Kyeyoung Park, an associate professor of anthropology at the Centre for Korean Studies at the University of California, Los Angeles. "Calling him a South Korean native, as if he arrived yesterday, doesn't make sense to me," she said. She called the gunman "American raised," having arrived there with his parents when he was eight years old.

I'm not sure what American raised meant, beyond geography. Cho's parents raising him in America were Korean. If America was America outside their home, then it was multicultural.

The lives of thirty-two students and teachers would not have ended that day had Cho Seung Hui never come to America, but instead of blaming immigration, we blamed Virginia Tech. In 2012, a jury found it negligent for delaying a campus warning after the first two shootings, which it believed were isolated.

Virginia Tech didn't defer to racism. The year after the massacre, Haiyang Zhu came there from China to study for a doctorate of philosophy in agricultural and applied economics. On the third Wednesday night in January 2009, in a campus café, he beheaded another student, Xin Yang, who'd arrived from China earlier that month. He loved her.

So, when Korean One Goh lined six female students against the wall at Oikos University in Oakland, California, the first Monday of April, 2012 and murdered them, before killing a man whose car he stole, there was no hint of a backlash against Koreans. The backlash was against America. "America has to look into its soul," chided Oakland mayor Jean Quan. "It cannot be that we can find more guns in our streets than we can find healthcare and mental health services. That cannot be. That's not our America."

She essentially blamed American governments, but not for

allowing interracial immigration. She blamed them for not banning guns or providing more healthcare.

If we're open to the possibility of there being differences between races, then it becomes reasonable to suppose that African, Middle Eastern, and Asian countries are autocratic because they need to be. The West didn't need to be, until other races came. Without tribal or religious authorities, governing some races (wherever they happen to be) requires more laws and policing than we'd spend governing our racially homogenous selves. If we're not going to free the aggression of other races, we must live without liberties we take for granted.

Without comparing cultures or belittling any religion, the only religions aside from Christianity that Western liberalism can accommodate are those that adherents keep close to their communities and those that aren't important. Islam is important.

In October 2012, the *Printemps de Septembre* art festival in Toulouse included projections of Mounir Fatmi's Islamic calligraphy onto the Pont Neuf Bridge. Being based upon verses from the Koran and sayings of the prophet Mohammed, Muslims demanded they not be walked upon. The projections were supposed to occur only at weekends, when cordons on the bridge would prevent pedestrians from walking on them. They were accidentally shown late Tuesday night, almost starting a riot.

Up to eighty young Muslims, many called in from the city's housing estates, quickly gathered on the bridge to stop pedestrians treading on the projection. They slapped one woman who inadvertently walked onto it, claiming she provoked them.

"Young people saw the projections and thought they were a deliberate insult," explained Hassan Idmiloud, vice president of the Toulouse Muslim Association. "We stepped in to explain that this beautiful work of art was actually homage to Islam, that it was a genuine mistake to project it on Wednesday before a cordon was in place."

The artist, "*a Moroccan of Muslim origin*" (which presumably meant he was Muslim) cancelled the projection of his work, called Technologia, owned by the Arab Museum of Modern Art in Doha, Qatar. "When it was shown there for the first time," he said, "just a few kilometres from Saudi Arabia, no one was shocked. That people were shocked in Toulouse is astonishing. I just don't get it." Another of Fatmi's works remained projected onto the façade of the landmark Hotel Dieu in Toulouse.

Free speech was a cornerstone of liberalism. It has proven incompatible with multiculturalism.

In spite of our best efforts, Muslims in the West constantly fear being insulted as they don't in Muslim countries. When we err by what might seem to us a trivial degree, their pride, faith, and collective identities (unimaginable to us) compel them to react, violently if need be. If we're not striving hard to overcome the complications of accommodating their culture, we're denying them.

Culture wasn't in mind when Playland Park, New York, banned hats and other headgear, coverings, and accessories from some of its rides so they didn't fall onto the tracks and derail the rides. "*All items and clothing must be appropriately secured while on a ride*," said its policy, "*some smaller items can be stored/secured in cargo pockets or waist pouches. Hats must be secured, and jackets/sweaters must be worn properly and not around the waist while on a ride. Some rides do not allow backpacks, purses or head gear of any kind.*"

The safety rule was in place without issue for four years until 2011, when large numbers of Muslims came to the park celebrating Eid-ul-Fitr, the end of Ramadan. Park officials had previously told the Muslim American Society of New York (which organised many of the visitors) about the ban on headgear, but still Muslims at the park were angry. "Everybody got mad, everybody got upset," said Brooklyn resident Amr Khater. "It's our holiday. Why would you do this to us?"

Muslims own their holidays. We don't even own ours.

"They knew about it beforehand," said a source at the park. "The organiser either didn't tell everyone or some people were angry about it already when they got here."

Park officials offered them refunds they didn't accept. A group of upset girls and women wearing hijabs began yelling at park security. Sixteen-year-old Lola Ali alleged the security officers started pushing them away, the girls stood their ground, and the security officers grabbed them, pushed them to the ground, and handcuffed them, when Muslim men intervened. "They were beating down the girls," Ali alleged of the security offices, "then they started beating down the guys."

Police rejected her claims, as did a park cashier who saw a woman wearing a hijab either push or hit a ride operator who forbade her from boarding the ride. A police officer tried to restrain the woman and the woman's husband took offence, at which point more Muslims joined the melee.

Thirty to forty park visitors became involved in the ruckus, in which two park rangers were injured. County police and officers from Mamaroneck village, Harrison, Port Chester, state police, and Metropolitan Transportation Authority police came in. Police arrested at least ten Muslims, mostly for disorderly conduct. Among sixty cruisers from various agencies at the park were three dozen cruisers blocking the entrance, while a helicopter flew overhead.

Intrinsic to multiculturalism are tensions that racial homogeneity doesn't suffer. Multicultural environments are innately more prone to violence, because the energy for which we enthuse becomes conflict whenever someone feels aggrieved.

9. ECONOMIC INCENTIVES

A rare instant of a nation voluntarily granting citizenship to other races before the Second World War was the *Constitutio Antoniniana* of 212 A.D. Emperor Caracalla extended Roman citizenship to all free men of the Roman Empire and offered all women the rights of Roman women, with some exceptions. Although *"Caracalla's motives may have had more to do with getting in more taxes than with idealism or generosity,"* wrote British historian Dame Averil Cameron in 1993, *"this measure extended the notion of what was considered 'Roman' to cover a multitude of ethnically and locally divergent cultures."*

It was a grant of legal rights and privileges. Rome seems not to have imagined societies encompassing more than one race.

In the sorts of conversations I have, a fellow said to me that societies always collapse after taking other races for their servants. The example he gave was Rome. Taking servants of some form or another was the only basis upon which any society allowed other races into their countries in any material numbers, until the West did after World War II. They remain a major plank of Western immigration programmes. We call them employees.

The West has become fixated with economics because we have to be, trying to give people reason to co-operate. The only interests individuals and races have in each other, the primary relationships between them, are commercial: earning money and spending it.

We're not countries. We're economies. We're not communities. We're commercial transactions.

A short time after hearing the principal address our children's primary school the Friday before Harmony Day 2011, I was in a bank at a nearby shopping centre. I waited impatiently for a South Asian teller so stupid as to need careful instruction from her fellow teller about something or other simple. I asked for five twenty-dollar notes, received two fifty-dollar notes, and never wondered what in hell such an idiot was doing there. It was her country too, apparently. It wasn't mine.

The only racial or religious integration is pecuniary. Some

people don't even have that.

Eritrean social activist Berhan Ahmed, head of the African Think Tank, told a 2011 Australian parliamentary inquiry into multiculturalism that Sudanese immigrants in Melbourne suffered boredom and lack of engagement. "Families are not getting anywhere," he said. "Their kids are also feeling that frustration." A month later, in April, Sudanese in Melbourne embarked upon three nights of violence. (They weren't bored or suffering a lack of engagement then.)

A man walking through the Church Street Mall, Parramatta at two o'clock the second Sunday morning of July 2011 heard cries for help from a fifteen-year-old girl being raped in a flower bed near a church. First news reports focused not upon the two rapists but on the girl walking alone late at night, as if she were to blame, and on the man ignoring her cries, although he was only exercising his rights to do as he pleased. I'm sure he'd have sold the rapists a knife or victim a box of tissues for prices good enough, but caring for our compatriots without good monetary reasons would be nationalistic. We don't do nations anymore. We're individuals.

Two days later, the rapists not having been caught meant that the *Australian Associated Press* news service mentioned them being of African appearance. Channel Ten *News* that evening didn't.

I first read of Ernie Friedlander's Harmony Day poster competition the Monday morning after the first weekend of August, 2011. That Saturday night, hundreds of young men had attacked police and burnt shops, police cars, and a double-decker bus in north London after police shot a father of four, Mark Duggan, the previous Thursday. Only one news report I saw mentioned that Duggan was black, although that was presumably because police had shot him. A handful of reports mentioned that he was a criminal who'd shot at police. One report referred to Duggan's friends and family initiating a protest march: tribalism at play, loyalty. One recalcitrant report described the subsequent riots as race riots.

A crumbled nation fuelled the mayhem, involving fifteen thousand rioters and consuming several English cities through five days and nights. "Looting tends to involve a wider range of people – children, women, older people – because it does not involve physical violence," said University of Leeds sociologist Paul Bagguley. "Riots enable people to lose their inhibitions, give them liberty to do things they wouldn't normally do."

Obsessed as we are with economics, economic factors are our favourite fingers of blame. "Without jobs people are more likely to be hanging around the streets," said Bagguley. They had time on their hands when trouble started.

Jobs occupy our minds, distracting us. Money lets us buy things to consume what remains of our time. Without them, we have only reality.

The onus of avoiding more violence by finding black people work was upon white people, even if few of us still lived in Tottenham. "*Successive British governments have colluded in incubating the poverty,*" complained Mary Riddell for London's *Daily Telegraph* newspaper, "*the inequality and the inhumanity now exacerbated by financial turmoil.*" (Western debt crises at the time hadn't caused rioting among merchant bankers.)

Riddell rejected the notion that race was a factor in the 2011 riots by suddenly acknowledging past riots (which until then, I'd forgotten) were racial, as we never did at the time. "*The Eighties uprisings at Broadwater Farm, as in Toxteth and Brixton, were products, in part, of a poisonous racism absent in today's Tottenham, where the Chinese grocery, the Turkish store and the African hairdresser's sit side by side.*"

Shopping is our parameter. Riddell's conclusion that race had vanished from Tottenham flowed from different races operating stores adjoining each other. Racial harmony means storekeepers not fighting each other. (Shoplifting is presumably fine.)

Economic transactions aren't society. Two or more transactions to which people are party are simply business relationships.

No expert I read imagined race being a factor in the 2011 riots. The *Sydney Morning Herald* newspaper impressively managed to post a series of photographs of the riots on the second Tuesday of August 2011 in which the only looter's face close enough to the camera to discern was white. Black looters weren't so delicate, proudly publishing pictures of themselves on social networking websites.

Instead of race, veteran parliamentarian David Winnick apportioned some blame upon the oft reported complaints of police racism. "There are accusations," he said, "we have heard it on the home affairs select committee, that black people are stopped and searched more often…"

Police were pilloried, without thought as to whether the

accusations were true or, if so, what motivated police to stop and search black people more often. The police officers with whom I've dealt have been models of integrity and decency. Police helping a black youth who'd been stabbed sparked the 1981 riots in Brixton. Police constable Keith Blakelock was brutally hacked to death during a protest march from the Broadwater Farm public housing estate in 1985. Nevertheless, following the 2011 riots, Britain would expend still more effort eradicating alleged police racism.

'These riots were about race,' countered London schoolteacher Katharine Birbalsingh in a *Daily Telegraph* article. 'Why ignore the fact?'

Birbalsingh described a presentation to pupils at her school by Trident, the Metropolitan Police Service unit set up to investigate and inform London's black community about gun crime. To scare the children, the photos were all black people shot. Afterwards, Birbalsingh approached one of the policemen and mischievously asked him what percentage of those involved in gun crime was black. *"I kid you not, but my question made this thirty-something white man who was, after all, trained to deal with the black community and its issues, turn pink."*

He told her that about eighty percent of gun crime was blacks against blacks. Of the remaining twenty percent, about three quarters involved at least one black person. On the whole, white people involved in shootings were from Eastern Europe. (I thought of the gypsies, although they're not white. Birbalsingh wasn't specific.) The policeman's numbers were crude without precise statistics (allowing us to dismiss them). *"Problems cannot be addressed unless people are willing to tell the truth,"* wrote Birbalsingh. *"As with so many other things in this country, we stick our heads in the sand and refuse to speak out about it."*

In response came a furore. *"Wrong, Katherine,"* wrote Brian Schoneker. *"We speak out about it and are labeled racists."*

Drago Harley was more interesting. *"It is racist to believe that black people should obey society's rules when they did not have a say in crafting them. Since black people did not get to decide whether rioting or looting is bad, then they should not have to face consequences for it. The same is true with Muslims. Blacks and Muslims should not have to face any penalties for anything because they do not understand right and wrong and they don't wish to. Anyone who tries to make a black or Muslim person obey white people's rules is just a racist."*

Leo S thought Harley was being sarcastic. Albert 8184 did not. *"Let's turn your logic against you Drago,"* he wrote. *"Why should the police and victims of rioting obey society's rules? Why don't we just declare open season on all non-whites and lynch them in retaliation? Why don't non-Muslims in Muslim countries have riots and kill all the Muslims and take over the countries? You are a barbarian. You are your own best critic, because the results of your philosophies are the best testimony against you. You are the REASON that people hold negative views of blacks."*

I hadn't imagined Harley was black. His words sounded very Western to me, explaining multiculturalism.

We eagerly seized upon white people among the rioters of 2011 to dissociate the looting and violence from race. No matter how many other races run amok for whatever reasons, we need just one white face to prove riots aren't reason to keep races apart.

White rioters were also cited in 1981 as proof at the time those riots in Brixton weren't racial. We acknowledge a racially troubled past, even a recent past, as we don't acknowledge a racially troubled present. Amidst riots in decades to come, we'll look back on 2011 to say they were race riots, to argue race is no longer an issue.

No other rioter received as much publicity as white Laura Johnson, educated in a grammar school and living in a nice home with a tennis court. Rich rioters aren't a reason to dismiss class differences as white rioters are reasons to dismiss race. Most telling about her wasn't her wealth, schooling, or amoral opportunism, but her feeling no ownership of multiracial Britain.

Fundamentally, racial pluralism leaves no race owning cities and countries. As Soviet communism demonstrated decades earlier, when everybody owns something, nobody does. The problem with places where everyone belongs is that no one belongs. Britain is nobody's country. No one has reason to care.

Amidst the rush of analyses of everything except race contributing to the riots was one equating the widespread destruction of 2011 with lesser riots of centuries past. Yet, we went through the Great Depression, wartime and post-war austerity, and other crises without the violence of 2011 because we had a sense of society, quite apart from whether we had jobs or shops were open to trade. We belonged by virtue of our race. Other races did not.

The British government commissioned the Riots Communities and Victims Panel, chaired by Darra Singh, to investigate the causes of the 2011 riots. Needless to say, there was no suggestion of race or multiculturalism being a factor. Instead, the culprits included bad parenting, unemployment, and schools failing to teach children to read and write. (Teachers were busy eradicating racism.) They were all supposed to give people a stake in society, which the report confirmed the rioters lacked. They had a *"sense of hopelessness."*

We think we create community with jobs, giving people a stake in economic society. It's not enough.

The panel's report also blamed consumer advertisements, with looters targeting goods they'd seen advertised. *"While no one individual brand is to blame, children and young people must be protected from excessive marketing."*

Criminologist John Pitts also blamed advertisements, suggesting many of the rioters were probably from low-income, high-unemployment housing estates. They *"quickly see that police cannot control the situation, which leads to a sort of adrenalin-fuelled euphoria – suddenly you are in control and there is nothing anyone can do. Where we used to be defined by what we did, now we are defined by what we buy."* (Before both, we defined people by race.) *"These big stores are in the business of tempting and then suddenly these people find they can just walk into the shop and have it all."*

We who understand only economies being important reduce rich people's crimes to greed and poor people's to poverty, but greed is unending and poverty relative. A rich person in one country might have less than a poor person in another. At least through the 1990s or so, more than seventy percent of poor people in America owned cars and more than ninety-nine percent had television sets. I imagined similar proportions among rich people in many African countries.

We arbitrarily define poverty in terms of a percentage of the population overall: the poorest ten percent or whatever. Our definitions ensure there will always be poor. If certain races are poorer than others and more criminal, then we expect governments to find them jobs, consequently categorising other people as poor. Statistics barely change.

In 2013, the words *"Harmony Day"* appeared on a strip of hands hanging across the reception desk of the O.R.S. Group offices (adjoining the offices in which I worked), servicing job seekers and workplaces. The next day, the hands had gone. Affixed to the wall by the door was a sign: "*Attention: Area under video surveillance.*"

My Chinese friend James Lee told me racial conflicts arise when people suffer economically. Inevitably, at least some people will feel that they are. Multiculturalism fails when the economic incentives for civic order run out.

10. GENEROSITY
WITHOUT GRATITUDE

With his enchantingly melodious song 'Imagine' in 1971, British musician John Lennon imagined a world without countries or religion. He reflected the view of many of his generation that without those distinctions between people, there'd be no conflict. There'd be only peace.

Lennon was murdered in New York in 1980. "He was a very different person back in 1979 and '80 than he'd been when he wrote 'Imagine'," said Lennon's last personal assistant, Fred Seaman, in the 2011 documentary *Beatles Stories*. "By 1979, he looked back on that guy and was embarrassed by that guy's naïvety."

We schoolboys through the 1970s made few conversations about anything too erudite, but my Jewish friend Gregor once remarked, "I don't even know why we need immigration laws." He spoke with bewilderment, and was the first person I heard question controls on immigration. Unlike people for whom open borders mean admitting immigrants into other people's neighbourhoods, Gregor couldn't comprehend why anyone couldn't live in his neighbourhood. Burdekin was very nice crescent.

The second Friday in February, 2009, Gregor and I were among six old school friends early that evening at Paddy Maguire's Irish Hotel. I wanted to stay there for dinner, but our Chinese friend Ted insisted we go to a restaurant he knew in Chinatown. "You can get a good meal for only fifty dollars," said Ted.

"We can do that here," I replied.

Everyone else deferred to Ted, who led us across George Street to the Emperor Gardens restaurant. Conversations again split into pairs and occasionally threesomes or foursomes.

Gregor had been proud and surprised his daughter had qualified for "O.C." at their local school. "You know what they say O.C. stands for?" he asked me.

"Opportunity classes," I replied, surprised he thought I hadn't known.

With Ted at the table, Gregor dipped his voice to explain, "Only Chinese."

We'd grown old enough to see and talk freely (at least with old friends) about the dysfunctional West in which we resided. I'd read only scant details of the murder of Omega Ruston, the father of two children, on Australia Day, a little more than two weeks earlier. Ruston's utility truck was flying Australian flags on the Gold Coast Highway when three people in a red or maroon sedan cut in front of him. The sedan pulled beside him near a Burleigh Heads bus stop and a gunman shot Ruston twice at close range. Three people from the sedan ran away.

The killing was blamed on "road rage." We blame all sorts of violence upon genres of rage. We don't blame criminals.

We blame victims. "I hope this will be a lesson to young people to be careful where they go," said Ruston's father, "and how they handle themselves."

Having seen no mention of the murderer's race, I was surprised to hear Gregor mention him being Lebanese. "Did they say the killer was Lebanese?" I asked him.

"No," replied Gregor, "but I put two and two together."

For all our efforts to remove reporting the races of criminals, a world of inference has developed. It is a netherworld that deduces certain races are more likely than other races to commit particular crimes, among all manner of matters we never say loudly.

The next morning I researched the matter. The murder had fallen quickly from the news, as most murders had come to do, but one long report the day afterwards mentioned the occupants of the car including a man of Middle Eastern appearance. The murderers were never caught, although police came to believe motorcycle gangs from Sydney were involved. Gregor was right.

The next time I saw Gregor, on the fourth Friday night in May, the Great Northern Hotel was far enough from Chinatown and, amazingly, from any of the many Chinese restaurants in Chatswood for Ted not to lead us away to eat. With Ted unable to hear him, Gregor talked passionately of Aborigines prejudiced against Asians, Japanese prejudiced against Koreans "and they look the same," and suburbs of Sydney in which white people had become minorities. One of his daughters had visited the elite private girls' school Pymble Ladies College to play sport, finding it "half Chinese, half

Indian." Like white people, Jews aren't all of one mind.

"You were the person," I reminded him, "who thirty years ago said we should have open borders."

He laughed. "I was naïve."

Living the 1960s dream, the West remains naïve. Only a fool opens his home to someone who'll steal his crockery. Only the naïve assumes nobody will. We're still playing John Lennon's song.

We imagine making everything fine with a hug. Being nice to warlords, telling them how lovely they are, we're sure they'll soon come around. We think thugs become angels when we give them houses and healthcare.

There'd been no Swedish empire and little colonial history, but a sense of humanitarian duty to the wider world when the parliament resolved unanimously in 1975 that racially homogenous Sweden would accept refugees and other immigrants from other races. She thought she'd overcome the problems of multiracialism in other countries by giving immigrants citizenship and generous government welfare benefits, while undertaking a plethora of programmes promoting racial integration. She presumed America's problems with Africans were a legacy of slavery, but all Sweden's immigrants would be free and voluntary.

Sweden was wrong. In 2008, rioters in Rosengaard in the southern city of Malmö set fire to cars and bins and clashed with police. They sparked riots in the Stockholm suburbs of Husby and Tensta.

By 2013, when more than fifteen percent of Swedish residents and twenty-three percent of Stockholm residents were immigrants and their families from outside the European Union, Prime Minister Fredrik Reinfeldt was confident that increasing employment had reduced crime and other social problems. The unemployment rate had fallen to eight percent in suburban Husby, where neatly kept flower beds and public gardens separated rows of clean housing blocks. An ornamental fountain, bars, shops, and a smart café bakery made the shopping precinct a picture-perfect image of multiracial Sweden.

Primarily from Turkey, the Middle East, and Somalia, immigrants amounted to more than eighty percent of residents in Husby. Responding to a Portuguese immigrant brandishing a machete, police were called to a flat one Monday night in May. Police negotiations failed, and they entered the flat to safeguard a woman there. The immigrant threatened to kill them, when police defending themselves killed him. Rami al-Khamisi, a law student and founder of the youth organisation Megafonen, called it police brutality.

News of the killing led young immigrants to riot for six nights, beginning the following Sunday. Riots spread to other suburbs of Stockholm such as Rinkeby, which experienced similar rioting in 2010. Immigrants set fire to up to two hundred cars, including more than a hundred on Sunday night alone. They stoned police officers and firefighters, including firemen trying to save a restaurant in Skogaas on Wednesday night. They set fire to buildings, including schools in Husby and Skaerholmen and a cultural centre in Husby, while bins burned across other suburbs. They damaged a police station and buildings in central Jakobsberg.

"We don't know why they are doing this," said Kjell Lindgren, a spokesman for Stockholm Police. "There is no answer to it."

"The problem is not from the Swedish government or from the Swedish people," said Swedish journalist Ingrid Carlqvist. "The last twenty years or so, we have seen so many immigrants coming to Sweden that really don't like Sweden. They do not want to integrate. They do not want to live in" Swedish "society: working, paying taxes and so on. The people come here now because they know that Sweden will give them money for nothing. They don't have to work, they don't have to pay taxes – they can just stay here and get a lot of money. That is really a problem."

Welcoming immigrants doesn't make them like us. Generosity doesn't make recipients into people donors want them to be, or presume they already are. No amount of money overcomes human or racial natures.

"In the old days, the neighbourhood was more Swedish and life felt like a dream," said Mohammed Abbas, who'd come as a refugee from Iran in 1994, "but now there are just too many foreigners, and a new generation that has grown up here with just their own culture."

Integrating immigrants is multiracialism without multiculturalism. Multiculturalism expects immigrants not to integrate. Both are unworkable in free democracies.

"We have tried harder than any other European country to integrate, spending billions on a welfare system that is designed to help jobless immigrants and guarantee them a good quality of life," lamented Marc Abramsson, leader of the National Democrats Party. "Yet we have areas where there are ethnic groups that just don't identify with Swedish society. They see the police and even the fire brigade as part of the state, and they attack them. We have tried everything, anything, to improve things, but it hasn't worked. It's not about racism. It's just that multiculturalism doesn't recognise how humans actually function."

The problems of interracial immigration don't become less with generations born in their new lands. They become worse. Even if we impose conditions upon immigrants coming into a country, their children feel no obligations. They don't even feel gratitude.

Rami al Khamisi's family escaped to Sweden from Iraq in 1994, but she believed Swedes were unreasonable to expect refugees to be perennially grateful for accepting them. She blamed the 2013 riots upon a "growing marginalisation and segregation in Sweden over the past ten, twenty years" from the perspectives of race and class. Refugees and their children expect more from the West than just refuge.

They've no need to appreciate the refuge, home, and money we grant them because we tell them they have rights. They've no cause to value them but every cause to demand more. Conversely, we don't sense our kindness towards them because we think we've done what we had to do. Their entitlement binds us.

Sweden remained the most generous country amidst the most generous continent on earth to immigrants, although I read as much blame for the riots upon the Swedish government recently reducing welfare entitlements as I read of blame upon rioters. They'd not worked to come and not worked for the money Sweden gave them on arrival. Expecting them to start working for their next benefit becomes unfair.

The more we give, the greater the recipients' expectations of getting more. Hearing us declare that everyone's equal, we encourage other races to expect everything their Western hosts enjoy. We've created expectations of equality, even among people not studying and working as hard as we do. People seeing others fare better than they're faring feel frustrated. The more they fall short of what we've assured them they deserve, living as we live, the more virulent their frustrations. People who could've been peaceful in their countries become criminals in ours.

"Anyone who wants to regulate immigration is immediately

classified as a nationalist, which also implies a racist as well," complained Aje Carlbom, a Swedish academic and author of a critical study into Swedish immigration policy, after the 2013 riots. "It is still almost impossible to debate this question."

We don't debate. We celebrate. Multiculturalism is a failed ideology, but we hang onto our multiracial ideals. Doggedly we refuse to let go of the dream.

"Sweden's centre-right coalition leaders should resist the temptation of undoing decades of enlightened social policy," lectured the editorial in Britain's *Guardian* newspaper. No amount of destruction or violence when multiculturalism goes wrong keeps us from feeling enlightened.

Sweden resisted the temptation. Immigration into Sweden increased.

Racial homogeneity means people are more likely to take responsibility for their lives. Racial diversity leads people to blame other races for their failings and misadventure.

Even if we redistribute all our wealth to make races equal, people aren't equal. A person from a dominant race not getting a job, prize, or anything else is more likely to hold his or her ability responsible. No matter how many successful people (even an American president) hail from a minority race, a black man failing to get a promotion will blame prejudice. So will an Islander woman without a dress as nice as one she saw on television. They're uninterested in their races' successes and other races' failures.

Black American Vester Flanagan accused 7-Eleven stores of being racist for selling watermelon-flavoured Slurpees. At television station WDBJ7 in Virginia, he accused white woman Alison Parker of racism because she spoke of "swinging" by a place and of a reporter being "out in the field," which Flanagan associated with cotton fields. The station dismissed him for poor performance, but he continued blaming racism for his failings. The last Wednesday in August 2015, while young white cameraman Adam Ward was filming even younger Parker interviewing a local businesswoman, he shot his two former colleagues dead.

The day of the shooting, Flanagan set out his desire to start a race war in a manifesto twenty-three pages long he sent to the American Broadcasting Corporation offices in New York. Journalists (who'd had so much to say about white American Dylann Roof's racial motives killing nine black Americans in a

Charleston church two months earlier) had nothing or next to
nothing to say about Flanagan's race. (Nor did Flanagan's
homosexuality get much of a mention.)

The only solution we imagine is winding back white racial
dominance. Then we can all blame prejudice for whatever we lack
that someone else has. We can all feel frustrated.

Our battle against race is a battle against reality: an unwinnable
battle we keep waging. If we're trying to demonstrate to the world
that we're all individuals and countries are superfluous, then half a
century after the West began racial integration, all we've shown is
that people are tribal and boundaries are necessary. The more we
admit interracial immigrants, the more we're accused of racism. If
we're trying to prove different races can live together freely and
harmoniously, then we're only proving they can't, not even with
our wealth and welfare payments.

Money doesn't engage people. It simply funds them.

Occasionally, we've toyed with undoing our multiracial
experiment: again respecting human nature rather than denying or
trying to change it. In 1977, the French government announced the
"aide au retour" (help to return), offering immigrants ten thousand
francs to return to their countries of origin. Only sixty thousand
went, most of them Portuguese and Spaniards instead of the North
Africans to whom the scheme was directed. For all their
complaints, life in France can't have been too bad for the North
Africans.

In December 2008, the Spanish government responded to the
highest unemployment rate in the European Union by offering to
pay unemployed foreigners to go home. Again, few accepted the
offer. I learnt of it in a news report about immigrants rioting across
Spain after three Moroccans stabbed a Malian in La Mojonera.
Media reports blamed the rioting on economic conditions.

The longer we take before properly untangling our multiracial
experiment, the more difficult it will be. The more expensive it will
have been.

11. POLICING

The Victorian Equal Opportunity and Human Rights Commissioner Helen Szoke complained in 2010 that young Africans felt targeted by police. Police were supposed to leave them alone.

Members of the African American and African Studies, Black Faculty and Staff Association, Black Graduate and Professional Student Association, Black Men's Forum, Black Student Union, and Huntley House for African American Males at the University of Minnesota wrote to university president Eric Kaler and vice president of university services Pamela Wheelock early in December 2013, objecting to the university using racial descriptors in crime alerts. (They didn't mind racial descriptors in faculty and student associations.) They insisted that *"efforts to reduce crime should never be at the expense of our Black men, or any specific group of people likely to be targeted. In addition to causing Black men to feel unsafe and distrusted, racial profiling is proven to inflict negative psychological effects on its victims."*

Those black men weren't victims of rape or other assault, but of feeling unsafe and distrusted. "The repeated black, black, black suspect," complained Ian Taylor, president of the Black Men's Forum in January 2014, "really discomforts the mental and physical comfort for students on campus because they feel like suspicions begin to increase."

The university retained the use of racial descriptors in crime alerts, because other universities did. It condemned racial profiling.

Police pleas for public help in finding suspects can require the most obvious descriptors of suspects' physical appearances. Race might get a mention, but only to an audience able to help.

While watching the film *Harry Potter and the Half-Blood Prince* in the Vue cinema, Leeds, with her husband and two children the last Sunday in July 2009, a woman asked a group of five or six teenagers to make less noise. That was a mistake. After the film, the teenagers abused her from their car. Fifteen minutes later, two of them followed her family to a Frankie & Benny's restaurant, where they threw bleach on her, burning her severely and risking permanent damage to her eyes.

The *Daily Telegraph* newspaper in faraway Australia reported the attackers only as teenagers. The *Australian* newspaper specified that one was a girl. The *Daily Mail* newspaper in England, whose readers might've been able to help police seeking the assailants, specified the two teenagers who doused the mother with bleach as being mixed race and Asian. The girl, who wasn't with them when the bleach was thrown, was black. Also not there when the bleach was thrown, the driver of the car was white. We had criminal diversity.

On the first Saturday of October 2008, Sydney newspapers reported a fifteen-year-old girl who'd been jogging through suburban Concord at a quarter past six the previous afternoon when a two-door hatchback car pulled up behind her. A man stepped from the car and talked to her, before grabbing her arm. When someone from the far side of the street yelled out, the girl broke free and ran away. *"Police say they are looking for two men of African appearance,"* said the *Australian Associated Press* news service. *"They say the one that got out of the car was aged about 25, of slim build, about 175cm tall with oily skin. He was wearing a dark T-shirt. The driver, aged about 25, was described as obese."*

The article went on to mention another attempted abduction the previous day, Thursday, in Liverpool, western Sydney. An eleven-year-old boy and his friend were leaving a leisure centre when a man stepped from a car and grabbed the boy by his shirt. The boy screamed and the man fled. *"Police want to question a man described as of middle eastern/Mediterranean appearance, tall with a slim build, aged between 40 to 50. He was wearing a brown shirt and cream or white pants."*

The following weekend, early on Saturday evening, a man offered three children cash to get into his car at Lethbridge Park. *"The man was described as being of Aboriginal appearance,"* reported *Australian Associated Press,* *"in his mid-20s, with a dark complexion, medium build and about 170cm tall. He was wearing a white t-shirt with black writing across the front and black knee-length shorts."*

The next weekend, early Sunday afternoon, there was no escape in Waterloo. A man followed a Chinese woman into the security building in which she lived. In the lift, he put a kitchen knife to her throat. He forced her to lead him into her third-floor apartment, where he kept her, a female friend, and her Chinese female and Korean male flatmates hostage. He raped the female flatmate, Liao Wei, three times and male flatmate twice. He forced all four of them to perform sexual acts on each other and upon him.

After more than an hour, the flatmates tried to escape by climbing naked from their balcony to another, when they fell thirty-five metres to the concrete footpath. Wei died, the Korean was critically injured, and the intruder fled. *"Police have described the attacker as 175cm tall,"* reported the *Daily Telegraph* newspaper, *"of solid build, with dark complexion. He was casually dressed, had short dark hair and aged in his 30s."*

The *Sydney Morning Herald* newspaper initially wasn't so discreet, describing the man police were seeking as being *"dark skinned."* A day later, with police still searching for the suspect, the newspaper no longer alluded to his race. *"More than 20 detectives from the homicide squad and Redfern local area have launched a hunt for the man, described as being in his mid-20s with a stocky build and wearing shorts, a T-shirt and runners."*

Whatever might be reported when police are searching for suspected criminals, all mention of their racial traits disappears when police apprehend them. Driving to work Thursday morning, 2CH radio reported the arrest of "a Sydney man" in relation to the killing. Unlike the Asian victims, the suspect's race was, in our parlance, irrelevant. We don't want white people thinking poorly of other races.

News reports that I heard, watched, and read only referred to him being a Sydney man twenty-six years old, while repeating his English-sounding name, Brendan David Dennison. When the matter came to court and he admitted the rape and murder, he became a *"homeless man."* A news network carelessly mentioned his lawyer was from the Aboriginal Legal Service.

There were instances of police looking for masked men or unseen suspects, but too many descriptions suggesting races other than ours for me to continue recording them. There's been no end of them since then, while my non-fiction writing popped in and out of matters of race. The proportion of suspected criminals from other races is much higher than their proportion of the general population, even the young population, warrants.

For fear their crimes might taint people's impressions of those races, race remains our last resort in describing a suspect: far below needing dental work. 'Sexual assault: woman fights off attacker with large overbite,' said one headline from the *Sydney Morning Herald*, the second Tuesday of May 2009. A woman walking through Merrylands Memorial Park at six fifteen the previous evening had been sexually assaulted. The assailant fled, but identifying him to the world only by his need for dental work, or even his red top, blue jeans, and white runners, was hardly going to help people recognise him. Near the end of the article, the newspaper mentioned the attacker was *"black or African appearance, about 190cm tall, aged in his early to mid-20s with a thin build and broad shoulders."*

The following day, on the Prospect Highway at Seven Hills, a woman stopped her car at traffic lights. A man approached the car, opened the door, and punched her. He demanded she give him her car, before two men in a white utility truck came to her aid. The man fled. *"A man of African appearance is wanted for questioning over the incident. He is about 183cm tall and of slim build. At the time of the incident he was wearing a black jumper, blue pants and white sneakers."*

He couldn't have been the man in Merrylands. There was no mention of him having an overbite.

More often than not, we water racial descriptions down to skin tones. Criminals can have brown or dark skin, much like white people who've sat in the sun.

Shortly after six o'clock the second Sunday of September 2010, in a crowd on Flinders Street railway station, Melbourne, a man followed a thirteen-year-old girl from Prahran. She stood on a downwards escalator, listening to her iPod, when he touched her from behind. They spoke briefly, when he touched the front of her body and walked off, before following her again. When she approached station staff, he fled onto a train. *"The man is described as being around 175 centimetres tall,"* said the last line of the *Age* newspaper report, since police wanted to speak to him, *"with average build, black hair, has dark skin and was wearing a navy blue shirt and black pants."* Gone were the days we spoke to strangers at railway stations.

Where we can rely upon something other than race, we do. Hair colour can be ideal, especially when it's unnatural. A streak of dye will suffice.

The *Sydney Morning Herald* reported a man in an unusual car following a teenage boy to school in Penrith at nine o'clock in the morning of the third Monday in July, 2011. At about three o'clock that afternoon, the same man and car followed the boy home. 'Hunt for the man with the souped-up car and the blond tips in his hair,' read the headline. Tucked into the article was a more complete description of the man not yet found. "*The driver appeared Middle Eastern or Mediterranean, about 170-175cm tall, with a large muscular build, olive complexion, short dark brown hair, spiky on top with blond tips. He had a small goatee beard and was wearing Nike shoes.*"

At about eleven o'clock the morning of 2011 Melbourne Cup Day, a man on the corner of Peel and Market Streets, North Melbourne, followed a woman into Peel Street and verbally harassed her. She told him to go away, whereby he forced her to the ground and sexually assaulted her.

Police looking for him described him "*as having a slim build with a dark complexion and dark eyes. He also had distinctive dark-coloured dreadlocks hair with orange tips at the end. He was wearing a dark coloured zip front hooded jumper at the time of the attack.*" The *Age* also included a photograph; what the police called a dark complexion, we used to call black. If there was uncertainty as to his race, it was because he could've been African or Aboriginal.

Hair is a particular favourite among our post-racial descriptors. In 2014, *News Limited Network* described the person of interest in the disappearance of University of Virginia student Hannah Graham as a man with dreadlocked hair, without mention he was black. She was later found dead.

Averting crime isn't reason for us to talk about race. At about nine o'clock in the evening of the third Sunday in February 2012, a gang of up to twenty men in Lakemba demanded a man give them some of his property. They then stabbed him. "*The group of men has been described as being of Mediterranean/Middle Eastern appearance,*" reported the *Australian Associated Press*. The *Sydney Morning Herald* omitted that sentence when it published the report.

"*In reporting crime,*" wrote radio presenter Madonna King in 2010, "*we are hesitant to say a group of Maori youths, or Chinese teenagers went on a rampage, or that police are searching for an Aboriginal man in connection with a crime. The very mention of it suggests we are targeting a whole race – yet by generalising, we might make it harder to find the culprit.*"

Our reticence about mentioning race allows problems for races to fester, which only bothers us when the races aren't ours. "*On Aboriginal affairs generally, political correctness has meant we have failed a generation of Indigenous people*," King continued. "*Aboriginal communities are riddled with domestic violence, alcoholism and crime. You even feel a bit guilty writing it.*"

King went onto fear for the future of mentally ill people for as long as they couldn't be talked about. "*And the rest of us will be too scared to order a black coffee.*"

A school liaison officer from the New South Wales police force visited my eldest daughter's high school her first year there, the last Tuesday evening in October 2010. Talking with school parents over supper, the policewoman lamented that "political correctness" wasn't just hampering the police in their job. It was also wrecking the country.

When pressed to explain, she said the people vandalising cars and other property on the Central Coast were Lebanese holidaying from Sydney. Away from home, the Lebanese thought no one would identify them. The damage they caused left a trail to the apartments at which they were staying.

Tony had been a Sydney policeman for eight years, stationed at Canterbury and Redfern, long before I met him on a mining industry cruise on Sydney Harbour in July 2011. When I mentioned to him that I was writing a book I then called *Harmony Day*, he replied: "Oh, Steal a Car Day."

He was a huge, solidly built man, with a bald head and no neck. Nevertheless, he said of tending to the Canterbury rugby league team home games, that "the Muslims were terrifying."

In the clash between harmony and saving the country, we want harmony. Faux harmony is better than none.

In 2010, police commissioner Karl O'Callaghan ordered Western Australian police to stop mentioning suspects' nationality, race, or religion when seeking public assistance to find them. Police could only describe a person as light or dark skinned. "More general descriptors limit the chances for people to make error," claimed police media spokesman Samuel Dinnison. (Police could've removed all chance of error by offering no descriptions at all.)

The Equal Opportunities Commission said the ban was introduced after complaints that ethnic descriptions were racist. Policing didn't come into it.

Six months after O'Callaghan's order, Western Australian Police Union president Russell Armstrong wanted police to be allowed again to mention a suspect's race, saying "scant descriptions" were making it harder to catch criminals and obstructing investigations. A police insider said being unable to mention suspects' race sometimes prevented their capture altogether.

Remaining unmoved, the Equal Opportunity Commission would investigate any incidents of police again using ethnic descriptions. "It can feed into prejudiced ideas in the community about which ethnicities are mainly responsible for criminal behaviour," said state commissioner Yvonne Henderson, no more interested in the best means to apprehend criminals than the reasons for prejudiced ideas in the first place. "Often they were inaccurate because they were based on one person's assumption of someone's racial background, which could be wrong."

"If police say they are looking for an Indian, how would the public know to distinguish between an Indian and a Pakistani?" concurred Ethnic Communities Council of Western Australia president Maria Saraceni, "It is much more accurate to use details like height, weight, or hair colour."

Indians, Pakistanis, and others from that racial region could be called "South Asians" or "sub-continental." Other critics have claimed the differences between Middle Eastern and Mediterranean appearances aren't clear, but the terms were normally applied together.

"The continued use of ethnic descriptors enforces stereotypes," chimed in police spokesman Bill Munnee, "does not promote understanding between cultures, damages police–community relationships, and is not considered a sound investigatory practice."

The police union considered the use of racial descriptors sound investigatory practice. Rather than risking racial disharmony, we let criminals go free, perhaps to commit crimes again. Understanding between cultures and police–community relationships depend upon police concealing the facts about crime.

Our police forces are careful not to offend other races, however prevalent crime is among them. Instead, we recruit them.

Minneapolis police and the mayor made much of appointing Mohamed Noor one of the first Somali police officers in Minneapolis. In July 2017, Noor, aged thirty-three, and another officer answered a report from forty-year-old white woman Justine Damond about the possible assault of a woman in an alley behind her home. Their police car patrolled the area, the other officer driving. After Noor reported the area as safe, Damond approached the car's driver-side window. From his front passenger seat, Noor drew his gun, pointed it past the officer beside him, and shot Damond dead.

Damond was a spiritual healer and meditation coach. She was engaged to marry the following month.

12. TOLERANCE

Protecting its people from crime has been cited as a reason that aging Japan doesn't allow other races to settle there, notwithstanding crimes Japanese commit. Japanese released Sarin gas into the Tokyo subway in 1995, killing a dozen Japanese.

Fundamentally, the West tolerates crime and terror. In October 2015, Victorian premier Daniel Andrews said "all of us…have to accept that violent extremism is part of a contemporary Australia."

In much the same spirit, my friend Karel shared on his Facebook computer page in September 2014 a cartoon in which a man watching a television programme hears the presenter ask, "What can we do to lessen the grip of fear from terrorism?" The man smiles, switching off his television set.

We have many reasons for indulging criminals and terrorists more than other races do. Our moral relativism leaves us without grounds upon which to judge people good or evil.

We're too individualistic to empathise with victims, satisfied simply that riots aren't erupting in the streets outside our homes, breaking our bedroom windows. We have no sense of being societies, races, or nations to defend. In the conflict between individual and collective interests, we hold steadfast to individuals, no matter how awful individuals are. The rest of the world favours societies. We could do the same by imagining victim societies made up of victim individuals, but don't.

Confined to a wheelchair, Canadian Heath Proden was waiting for a train on Mount Druitt railway station the second Tuesday evening in March 2010. Two teenagers approached him and abused him. He tried to flee but one punched him in the face, knocking him from his wheelchair. They then stomped on him, hitting his head and body with metal bars, one of which came from his wheelchair. They tried to steal his wheelchair and other belongings before leaving. They soon returned, bashing him with the bars from his wheelchair. Early news reports, before the second assailant was caught, mentioned he was a Pacific Islander.

Equating the attack to the snowmobile accidents that paralysed Proden and killed his stepfather ten years earlier, the *Sydney Morning Herald* newspaper blamed it too on *"fate,"* as if there were such a thing. We think we can't do anything about crime, but if Proden's injury was a turn of fate then it was multiracial fate: our multicultural burden. If that Islander, and almost certainly those two Islanders, had still been on their Pacific Island, they'd not have attacked Proden. They might've attacked someone there, but Western victims are no less victims for taking the places of victims from other races.

Through it all, we cosset criminals because proportionately so many more of them are from other races. Attendees at a small forum in the West Ryde Leagues Club in 2000 opposed new Northern Territory laws mandating minimum sentences for criminals in certain circumstances because so many people convicted of crimes were Aboriginal. "I don't think we should change our opinion of a law, because it disproportionately affects particular races," I told them, retaining a quaint view of the world.

In our determination to be kind, we forgive. We forget. Racial tolerance demands we tolerate crime.

In 2011 and '12, black students without disabilities were three times more likely than white ones to be expelled or suspended from American schools, according to government civil rights data. More than half the students arrested or referred to law enforcement were Hispanic or black. *"In short,"* the American Education and Justice Departments responded in a letter early in 2014, *"racial discrimination in school discipline is a real problem."*

They said principles of fairness and equity demanded that schools cease being so concerned with discipline. Instead, they should train teachers in conflict resolution. Schools failing to do so faced strong reprimand.

We don't discipline children. We discipline schools.

White students numbered only thirty percent of the students in the Minneapolis public school system. Other students were ten times more likely to be suspended from school. Thus from November 2014, Minneapolis Public Schools required schools to obtain permission from the school superintendent Bernadeia Johnson, a black woman, before suspending any black, Hispanic, or American Indian student for reasons other than violence.

In the five years from 2010, schools in St Paul paid almost three million dollars to the Pacific Educational Group to teach children that the American education system was built around white culture, tradition, and social norms to the detriment of black students. Misbehaving special-needs students were brought into regular classrooms. School officials began forgiving or ignoring violence and other previously unacceptable behaviour. "Time outs" replaced student suspensions.

"I think we're telling these kids you don't have to be on time for anything," said Becky McQueen, an educator at Harding High School, "we're just going to talk to you. You can assault somebody and we're gonna let you come back here."

They did assault people, time and again. "A significant number of families are saying their children do not feel safe in the schools," said Joe Nathan, executive director of the Centre for School Change in Minneapolis. "They don't feel safe even going to the bathroom."

By 2015, the American Education Department's compulsory Civil Rights Data Collection project was compiling information on student suspensions and expulsions by race from every public school district in America. Districts showing disparities in discipline would be forced to revise their discipline policies. (That is to say, to relax them.)

Rather than refusing to recognise race, we let other people's races mitigate. Justice can see after all.

When a Korean beat his young sister-in-law with a metal vacuum cleaner pipe, a hard plastic pipe, and a pop handle for not completing her homework fast enough, the District Court in Brisbane in 2009 acknowledged "cultural differences" between Koreans and Australians. For beatings that would have gaoled an Australian, the Korean escaped with a suspended sentence.

We're most forgiving of crime when white people are victims. Tomas Getachew was a teenager when he came to Australia as a refugee from Ethiopia in 2002. Five years later, he raped a woman he'd met at a social function. Five months after that, while working as an unlicensed bouncer at a hotel, he followed several recent school leavers to a beach and assaulted them. In 2009, a judge excused Getachew's lack of remorse for the "ugly and vicious" rape and other assaults, because of his experiences in Ethiopia.

The judge believed there was a good chance of rehabilitating Getachew. Responsibility for his rehabilitation was ours.

Refugees raping women aren't a reason for us to refuse them asylum. It's a reason for more compassion and understanding (although not for the women).

Several news reports described a teenager randomly attacking schoolboys in Brisbane with a meat cleaver. He inflicted a gash three inches long to one boy's cheek so deep that it reached a bone. He slashed another boy's back narrowly missing his spinal cord. Only when the Brisbane District Court passed sentence in 2010 did I learn Zinajdo Hasanovic had been a refugee from Bosnia. Judge David Searles reduced his sentence because Hasanovic's father and uncle dying in the Bosnian war when Hasanovic was young meant he was suffering post-traumatic stress disorder. (Unable to fathom the Bosnian's unprovoked maiming of two schoolboys, we knew he must have been mentally unwell.)

Immigration lawyer Kerry Murphy (a friend of mine at law school) expressed rather well our determination not to let the harm refugees do our countries deter us from granting them admission, welfare, family reunions, and everything else. "*Burning of property, and alleged assaults are serious and not to be condoned,*" Kerry wrote, a little pompously, in 2011. "*However, they are not so serious as to warrant someone not getting the full benefit of refugee protection.*" Nothing could be serious enough for that.

The cultural differences we're supposed to celebrate can be difficult for immigrants. Their crimes against white people become cultural misunderstandings.

In 2010, the dress and behaviour of women walking through public areas of Melbourne agitated Almahde Ahmad Atagore. Within a month after arriving in Australia, the Libyan sexually attacked seven of them, the youngest only twelve or thirteen years old. Judge Margaret Rizkalla in the Victorian County Court gaoled him for only five years and three months, accepting there'd been a link between the cultural issues, Atagore's depression, and the attacks.

Refugee Esmatullah Sharifi came from Afghanistan to Australia on a temporary protection visa in 2001. (Australians were the ones needing protection.) One night in December 2008, he drove from his home in Tullamarine to Frankston looking for a victim. He found an intoxicated woman sitting alone on the footpath near the 21st Century nightclub. Sharifi sat beside her, talked kindly to her, and learned she'd had a disagreement with friends. He offered to drive her to the hotel in Mornington where her friends had gone. She accepted, but he drove in a different direction. Becoming concerned, she sent a message through her mobile telephone to her friends, but he took her telephone. He found a dark street where he stopped. She cried and asked if he planned to kill her. Sharifi put his hand around her neck, forced her to remove her clothes, and raped her.

Five days later, on Christmas Eve 2008, Sharifi abducted and raped a woman in Melbourne. Even after seven years in the West, cultural differences with Afghanistan meant he had what a psychologist called "an unclear concept of what constitutes consent in sexual relationships."

In 2012, Sharifi's defence to that second rape charge was being a traumatised Muslim Afghan refugee. Lacking cultural sensitivity, Judge Mark Dean refused him. The Court of Appeal held the judge had erred. It reduced Sharifi's minimum sentence from eleven to eight and a half years because of his traumatic upbringing, ruling that Sharifi's resultant stress, depression, and anxiety increased "the burden of imprisonment upon" him.

Indulging other races isn't racist. It's racial sensitivity.

James Savage (born Russell Moore) robbing, sexually battering, and strangling American woman Barbara Ann Barber in 1988 wasn't newsworthy, so far as I noticed, until a Florida appeals court excused Savage from the death penalty for the anguish his life had been. He'd been among the Aboriginal children that Australian governments removed from their parents because their parents were neglecting them, whereby a kind and well-meaning white Salvation Army family adopted and cared for him. He entered reform school at the age of fifteen, where his unfortunate life became filled with drugs, alcohol, crime, and incarceration. A psychiatrist testified Savage felt out of place as a black person living among white people.

Crime is inevitable amidst multiculturalism. It's also excusable.

Aborigines numbered two percent of the New South Wales population in 2009. They comprised twenty-nine percent of prisoners in the state's gaols. In another time and context, I heard a speaker on the radio insist the state's justice system must be racist. Otherwise, the high rate of Aboriginal incarceration made Aborigines the most criminal race on earth.

Walking along a footpath in Kings Cross, Sydney, one evening in 2012, eighteen-year-old Thomas Kelly had every reason to presume his life ahead of him would be happy and successful, until he was one of four strangers that Kieran Loveridge punched that night after consuming a carton of double-strength vodka drinks with three others. Kelly died, causing much talk of alcohol-fuelled violence and creating a safe zone for young people at Kings Cross. His grieving family established the Thomas Kelly Youth Foundation.

Loveridge's name left me to presume he was Australian, until retired Aboriginal magistrate Pat O'Shane defended him as "an ordinary, everyday lad" in 2013. O'Shane didn't normally speak up for white people.

"I don't know why she felt she was compelled to make those comments," replied Kelly's father, properly oblivious to race.

I looked into Loveridge without finding reports of his race, but finding reference to his lawyer being Steven Rees from the Aboriginal Legal Service. O'Shane claimed alcohol-fuelled violence had been a major issue for two centuries, presumably referring to the period since Europeans came. She said gaol wasn't the answer for people like Loveridge, presumably meaning Aborigines.

In *Bugmy's Case*, 2013, the Australian High Court ruled that criminal courts must have regard to race in sentencing Aborigines, the so-called Fernando Principles, but only in their defence. The court held that race doesn't diminish in significance over time, not even for repeat offenders. Felicity Graham from the New South Wales Aboriginal Legal Service believed the ruling could reduce the number of Aborigines in prison.

It wouldn't reduce Aboriginal crime. It would reduce Aboriginal imprisonment.

Bugmy's lawyer, Stephen Lawrence, rejected the view that Aborigines received a racial discount. "In fact completely to the contrary, the arguments are about ensuring equality before the law through paying close attention to the background circumstances of people," he said. "It's actually necessary to examine difference, to understand difference, in order to achieve real equality."

That was to say, races being unequal, equality demands we treat races unequally. Equality requires racism.

When Silas Gordon Haines and Nathan Dungay were convicted of holding several students hostage, raping a Chinese woman, and assaulting two Vietnamese men after breaking into a townhouse in

Coffs Harbour in 2008, the news report focused upon the victims' races. "You're international," Haines told the woman, "I can give you Australian."

Sentencing Haines and Dungay in 2010, the judge took into account "their Aboriginal background." It reduced their punishments.

"*Unless acts of 'affirmative action'…are formally recognised,*" said the District Court's Judge Stephen Norrish in a paper to a justice reform conference in 2011, "*…the disproportionate number of Aboriginal people in the criminal justice system…will increase, to this nation's greater shame.*" He proposed recognising cultural and social circumstances as mitigating factors during sentencing, offering greater options to imprisonment for Aborigines, and not sending them to prison for terms of less than twelve months. The Bar Association agreed. Norrish also wanted circle sentencing, Koori courts, and Aboriginal prisons with a "*culturally appropriate…setting.*"

Even victims advocate Howard Brown liked Norrish's ideas. He called for criminal trials to consider Aboriginal culture and language.

While shadow attorney general Greg Smith rejected Aboriginality being a reason to reduce gaol sentences, he too considered the Aboriginal imprisonment rate "a disgrace," but not upon Aborigines. It was our disgrace.

In year eight, my second daughter's geography teacher told her class of the racism that gaoled Aborigines. "They haven't done anything wrong," she insisted, as if none should be in gaol.

Everything wrong with other races being our fault can become tiresome. "*What about some collective remorse and self-criticism from the Aboriginal community?*" asked journalist Paul Sheehan in 2011. "*What about the gangs of young Aboriginal men who roam the streets of Sydney and country towns stealing and belting white kids, a problem my extended family has experienced first-hand multiple times? What about an apology from the Aboriginal people (a concept which itself is a white fiction) for the endemic child abuse inside Aboriginal families and communities?*

"*I don't believe most Australians feel 'shame' that Aborigines are 15-times over-represented in the criminal justice system. I believe they feel anger, as the victims of crime. Australians are sick of the chasm between rhetoric and reality, and the idea that the only acceptable public narratives for Aboriginal people are that of victim or artist or noble custodian. The percentage of incarcerated Aboriginals would be even higher if so many were not given a free pass by the justice system, which in turn has led to a self-perpetuating culture of violence…*

"*Judge Norrish does not treat Aborigines as human beings. Instead they are to be treated as something outside Australian law and culture, as victims, mendicants, piccaninnies, avatars of white guilt, incapable of knowing right from wrong. His comments are profoundly insulting to the majority of Aboriginal and part-Aboriginal people who function well within the norms of society.*"

13. BIOLOGICAL BASES OF CRIMINALITY

Studying Medicine for less than a year after I finished school, a lecturer made the unremarkable observation that people living near large numbers of immigrants have more passionate opinions about them than people living near fewer immigrants. The less we encountered other races, the less we felt about them.

During the 1990s, Australian immigration minister Philip Ruddock rejected calls for the government to carry out a media campaign promoting tolerance of immigrants, because such a campaign in Europe exacerbated racism. He offered no explanation, but the reason might have been that the campaign confronted Europeans accustomed not to thinking of other races.

The Challenging Racism: The Anti-Racism Research Project survey, reported in 2008, revealed that forty percent (a very low figure by international standards) of Australians believed that some races didn't belong in Australia. The proportion was highest in New South Wales, where there were most immigrants, and least in the Australian Capital Territory, where there were fewest.

A man and his friend were walking across a three-metre-high bridge from Mawson Street to Cabramatta Avenue, Miller, New South Wales, at about eight twenty the second Wednesday evening of November 2010. Five Pacific Islander men confronted them. They argued before starting a fight, in which the Islanders threw the man from the bridge into Cabramatta Creek. He returned to the bridge, where the Islanders again punched and kicked him before fleeing.

While the victim lay in a coma in Liverpool Hospital, with swelling to his brain and fluid on his lungs, forty or so readers commenting on the news report blamed educational standards, the law, and society, but not the criminals. They didn't so much as mention them being Islanders, although the newspaper website moderator might've refused to publish comments that did.

Yet in 2009, Sydney Samoan Council representative Richard David acknowledged fundamental psychological differences between races, while blaming Australian referees for violence by Islanders and Lebanese at rugby league games. "The Polynesian instinct is very different to a European's," he said. "Our nature is not to speak and talk through our feelings, it's about the physical emotion and sometimes that can manifest in different ways." Describing (in such abstract terms) the assaults that led Parramatta Referees Association president Alan Shortall to threaten strike action, he made Islanders thumping people sound perfectly reasonable.

The science of epigenetics examines environmental impacts upon human brains, regulating the expression of innate genetic codes. Neuroscientist Adrian Raine knew in 1987 that Nazi eugenics more than forty years earlier still prevented consideration in his native Britain of biological bases for criminal behaviour.

After Richard Dawkins, author of *The Selfish Gene*, persuaded him to the "all-embracing influence of evolution on behaviour," Raine moved to America and began scanning the brains of murderers in prisons, using positron emission tomography. He found reduced activity in the prefrontal cortex (controlling emotional impulse) and greater activity in the amygdala (generating emotion). He also found that childhood abuse caused damage to the front of the head, possibly resulting in more rage and anger.

Raine presented a paper to his peers in 1994 showing a combination of birth complications and early maternal rejection of babies had significant correlation with individuals becoming violent criminals eighteen years later. Critics denounced his work as "*racist and ideologically motivated.*" *Nature* magazine reported that "*the uproar surrounding attempts to find biological causes for social problems will continue.*"

Fifteen years after first proposing a book describing some of his scientific findings, Raine finally published *The Anatomy of Violence* in 2013. By then a professor at the University of Pennsylvania, his work linked genetics and brains with criminality, while acknowledging environmental factors might play a role.

An autopsy in 1966 revealed Charles Whitman suffered from a tumour in the hypothalamus part of his brain. Highly intelligent (with an intelligence quotient, or I.Q., of 138), he'd been an eagle boy scout, member of the United States Marine Corps, and owner of a cache of guns, rifles, and pistols. On the first day of August 1966, he entered the Bell Tower of the University of Texas, from which he shot dead sixteen people and wounded more in a horrific murder spree. It became the subject of the only Harry Chapin song I don't enjoy, 'Sniper'.

David Eagleman, director of neuroscience and law at Baylor College in Texas, published *Incognito: The Secret Lives of the Brain* in 2011. He believed that brain tumours could cause criminal behaviour. Eagleman was Jewish.

In 2014, physician Jari Tiihonen of the Karolinska Institute in Stockholm and others reported their examinations of two separate cohorts of Finnish prisoners. They attributed around five to ten percent of violent crime in Finland to a monoamine oxidase A genotype and the CDH13 gene, linking that genotype and gene to at least ten homicides, attempted homicides, and batteries.

"I have heard about the so-called Warrior Genes and we can add these to the psychiatric illness genes, alcoholic genes, and obesity genes," responded Matthew Bambling, senior lecturer in psychiatry at the University of Queensland, in 2015. "Perhaps there is a gene for everything?" He nevertheless believed people could often control their behaviour, overriding their genes, if they wished. "The best research suggests that in most cases we are well able to override our behavioural genetics with our minds." (Clearly, many people don't.) "Environment is most important for most cases."

"If you've the high-risk form of the gene and you were abused early on in life, your chances of a life of crime are much higher," said professor in psychiatry at the University of California, Jim Fallon. "If you have the high-risk gene but you weren't abused, then there really wasn't much risk. So just a gene by itself, the variant doesn't really dramatically affect behaviour, but under certain environmental conditions there is a big difference."

We don't care. Still scarred by Nazism, we refuse to link criminality to genes or human physiology even where there's no correlation with race, unless the race is ours. Journalist Sherine Conyers wondered in 2015 whether Australia's origins as a penal colony could make "*Australia more likely to breed criminals.*"

When my second daughter complained about the aggressive and obnoxious girls of Carlingford High School, after a sports day between it and her school the fourth Wednesday in August 2012, I theorised all manner of social and economic explanations for the decline of a suburb I'd often visited many years earlier. Only after our long discussion did my daughter, most improperly, mention,

"They were all blacks and Asians."

Before the Old Knox Grammarians Association annual general meeting in 2013, James, the association auditor (and our parish Anglican church treasurer), was impressed that Knox boys sounded the same, whatever their race. It was our confidence that education created equality: we could overcome race.

James' words came to mind a month later as I read of North Korean tyrant Kim Jong-un having attended the International School of Berne from the age of eleven in 1994 until 1997. "Everyone now looks at him as a lunatic who hates the world," said former classmate Tal Rapp in 2013, "but the kid I remember was the quietest person I have ever met." As a schoolboy in Switzerland, Kim loved comics and American films like *Jurassic Park*. He played a member of the good gang, the T-Birds, in a performance of the American musical *Grease*. None of it prevented him from later threatening nuclear war against America and other countries in 2013.

Several future despots threatening the West enjoyed Western tutelage in their youth. In 1966, long before coming to power, Muammar Gaddafi studied at the Royal Army Education Corps Centre at Wilton Park, Beaconsfield. "There was apparently nothing that set him apart from the other students," said his former tutor Roy Hurst in 2011. "He was a young guy who didn't stand out from the crowd." As Libyan leader in 1988, he killed hundreds of Westerners aboard a Pan Am flight and in Lockerbie, Scotland.

The director of the Australian Institute of Criminology, Adam Tomison, saw no need for police to identify a criminal's "racial background," which presumably meant race, in 2010. "Justice is meant to be blind," he said, "and police are expected to investigate crimes…regardless of the circumstance and regardless of the victim or offender's cultural background or nationality." The more we reduced race to cultural background the less relevant it seemed, but with a significant proviso. "At present Australia's criminal justice system records the Aboriginality of offenders and victims as a means of identifying involvement with the criminal justice system, and in order to inform responses to this issue in a culturally sensitive way."

We're recording more race than just Aboriginality. Sitting beside me on a Sydney suburban train headed home the last day of April

2009 was a tall, thin man closely studying several pages of computer-printed text. Trying not to be noticed, I read as much of the uppermost page as I could. (We can learn all sorts of things reading other people's papers and computer screens on trains.) It related to the Violent Risk Information screen, designed to assist J.J.C. staff in the management and supervision of young offenders. The next morning, I used my computer to discover that J.J.C. referred to a New South Wales Juvenile Justice Centre, but found very little information about it or the V.R.I.

The page I'd read was headed with the details of a young offender, with entries for a *"Person I.D."* (identification), *"Full Name"*, *"D.O.B."* (date of birth), *"Gender"*, *"Alias,"* and *"Ethnicity."* The offender's name, alias, and ethnicity were all blacked out (which is probably the wrong phrase to use in this context). There was no compunction about revealing an offender's date of birth or gender along with his or her identification number (a very long number).

Somebody compiling the criminal profiles thought race was sufficiently relevant to include it in the database. If an offender's race was recorded purely to identify him or her in the future, then height, build, and other distinguishing features would also have been included. They weren't.

Adding to our difficulties is how little we know. In Britain, charities such as Barnardo's won't discuss the races or religions of criminals. The Home Office refuses to compile statistics about them. For all our decades of multiculturalism, we have no data at all.

In 1996, the Swedish National Council for Crime Prevention reported North African immigrants to be twenty-three times more likely to commit rape than Swedish men. Sweden didn't cease interracial immigration. Instead, over the ensuing decade or two, she ceased compiling criminal statistics according to race and ethnicity.

France banned the creation of racial files altogether, quite apart from matters of crime. Whatever relationship race might have with anything, there isn't to be one.

Computer search engine Google's algorithm automatically suggests words that users might intend when typing in letters and words to search, based upon what previous users have searched. S.O.S. Racisme, France's Union of Jewish Students, and the

Movement against Racism and for Friendship among Peoples sued Google in 2012 because the suggestions for businessman Rupert Murdoch and actor Jon Hamm included *"Jewish."* Neither man was Jewish, but large numbers of people had investigated whether they were. *"Numerous users of the premier search engine in France and the world confront daily an unsolicited and almost systematic association between the term 'Jewish' and the last names of prominent figures in politics, media and business,"* said the suit, suggesting Jewish *"omnipotence in the French leadership."*

Google's impartial algorithms again caused a problem in 2013. Latanya Sweeney, a professor of government and technology at Harvard University, reported the results of a study of more than two thousand names associated with particular races entered into the Google and *Reuters* websites. She found that names given to black babies, such as DeShawn, Darnell, and Jermaine, generated advertisements suggesting a record of police arrest in eighty-one to eighty-six percent of searches on one site and ninety-two to ninety-five percent on the other.

Names "predominantly given to white babies," such as Geoffrey, Jill, and Emma, generated such advertisements in only twenty-three to twenty-nine percent of searches in one site and zero to sixty percent in the other. They tended to generate advertisements with more neutral connotations, such as *"Looking for Emma Jones."*

"There is discrimination in delivery of these ads," Sweeney concluded. She said the study "raises more questions than it answers."

Google responded with a statement that its algorithm *"Ad Words does not conduct any racial profiling. We also have a policy which states that we will not allow ads that advocate against an organisation, person or group of people. It is up to individual advertisers to decide which keywords they want to choose to trigger their ads."*

Race remains relevant whenever people of another race plead it in their defence, to excuse otherwise unpalatable actions or idleness. New South Wales conducted three public inquiries in six months into Chinese attempting to bribe state government officials. (Whatever else immigration has done, it's been a boon for public inquiries.) When Jin Hua Chen and Yu Ling Sun came before the third inquiry, in May 2009, they tried to excuse their action as some sort of "cultural baggage."

Yiyan Wang of the Department of Chinese Studies at the University of Sydney confirmed that corruption was more common in China than Australia, but dismissed any suggestion of it being a racial affair because Australia wasn't free of corruption. There were in Australia, she said, simply more people "looking over your shoulder."

We agree. At one level, we don't contemplate that some races could be more criminal than others because crime isn't exclusive to any. There could be a thousand times more wrongdoers from another race than ours, but all we need to dispel any link between race and crime is a criminal who isn't of that race. (Finding someone of that race who isn't a wrongdoer might be too difficult.)

At another level, everyone from another race being bad wouldn't sway us. We still wouldn't notice. We reject any link between race and crime (unless the race is Western and the crime is our past imperialism, racism, and so forth) because we reject racism.

In the ethos of multiculturalism, we link wrongdoing not to race but to racism. If I read of Colin Ferguson killing six and wounding nineteen passengers on the Long Island Rail Road in 1993, I soon forgot it. Twenty years later, I stumbled upon reference to congresswoman Carolyn McCarthy's husband having been among the dead. Ferguson's legal defence team argued he'd suffered temporary insanity due to black rage brought upon by years of racial prejudice, without specifying that prejudice. Ferguson rejected the defence, claiming not to have committed the killings anyway.

Infuriated by the French government deporting gypsies en masse in September 2010, the Council of Europe wouldn't have a bar of claims they'd brought soaring crime rates. "Now we need all governments to come together," said secretary general Thorbjørn Jagland, "and agree the obligations that we have towards the Roma."

That same month, the Harghita Criminal Court in Romania tried twenty-six gypsies from Tandarei for human trafficking offences, money laundering, firearms offences, and membership of local organised crime clans. Large homes appearing among the gypsies had attracted police attention, leading investigators to learn that gangs had snatched a hundred and eighty-one poor Romanian children, ranging in age from a few months to seventeen years old.

The gypsies beat them, disfiguring some so they could earn more money, before sending them to Slough in England to wash car windscreens, beg, pick pockets, and steal from shops, giving the proceeds to their captors. Their cache included cash, jewellery, motor cars, AK-47 assault rifles, and grenade launchers.

Blaming immigrant crime upon Western intolerance couldn't be more preposterous. We assume people born in the West become like us even if their immigrant parents aren't, but nine hundred years in Europe haven't made the Roma less gypsy.

14. IDEOLOGICALLY ACCEPTABLE ASPECTS OF CRIME

Sometime soon after four o'clock the last Monday morning in October 2008, I was surprised to see a *News Limited Network* caption blame racial feuds for the growing violence in Victorian government schools. A dozen attacks occurred a week, often involving knives and machetes, with victims as young as six years old.

When next I saw the website, at about nine o'clock in the morning, that article was headed 'Class War in State Schools.' An error by someone at the night desk had been corrected, although tucked in the midst of the article remained a reference to racial feuds. Class warfare, colourless conflict, is an acceptable discussion point. Racial feuds aren't. Fixated with racial and religious harmony, we're uninterested in other harmony.

We equate prejudice with conflict, but when we face racial and religious prejudice manifest in conflict, we consider only the conflict. For a school assignment the third Monday in June 2013, my second daughter examined the problems students could experience researching the September 2001 terrorist attacks on America. She feared she could get in trouble from her teacher for her answers, particularly after I suggested one problem was the West's reluctance to talk candidly about Islam.

She wrote only of people's reluctance to speak of the issues, but still she worried. She soon abandoned her effort altogether, choosing another topic.

With any unlawful or socially undesirable action, there are two distinct lines of inquiry and response. The first focuses upon the individual perpetrator and any accomplices directly or indirectly involved. The second looks to broader factors that might have contributed to those perpetrators and accomplices acting as they did. With the latter, we consider all sorts of political, social, and economic forces, such as the treatment of women and children, social isolation as we imagine poor people have, and poverty, but we've disallowed race as a reason for anything bad. The only causes of crime we contemplate are environmental, but not multiculturalism.

"*A careful statistical analysis of the propensity to commit crimes would have to take into account a whole host of demographic, economic, and sociological considerations,*" wrote economist Sinclair Davidson of the Institute of Public Affairs in 2011. Arguing the relevance of age, income, and employment opportunities, he never wondered whether they correlate with race. "*It is very unlikely that country of birth would emerge as an indicator of criminality once other factors are accounted for. At first glance, it does appear that some small foreign born groups are over-represented in the Australian prison population – but that is likely to be a statistical artefact and not an indicator of criminality.*"

I don't know what a statistical artefact is. Davidson dismissed a statistic that Sudanese were four and a half times more likely than white Australians to be convicted of murder, essentially because only eleven murderers and just seventy-seven prisoners overall in Australian prisons in 2009 were Sudanese. "*The blunt reality is that the overwhelming majority of convicted criminals in Australian prisons are Australian born.*" In short, there weren't enough Sudanese in the country to be a crime wave.

(Davidson referred to Sudanese criminals as "*individuals*" throughout his argument, for fear anything else might lead to generalisation. Only good immigrants we call a community.)

Certain that different races can live together, we look for something other than race or multiculturalism to blame for crime. Through the four decades after Sweden chose to become multicultural, rates of violent crime increased four times. Rates of rape rose more than fifteen times to the second highest in the world. In spite of all the evidence that Muslim men were responsible for the increases, Swedish politicians blamed the rise in rape upon gender equality provoking Swedish men.

While the West denies race and culture, we're obsessed with gender. Thus we blamed Swedish men for the crimes of immigrant men.

The West defines criminals by their age and gender, but not race. We think it's perfectly reasonable to consider young men more unruly than elderly women, but completely irrational to consider young black men more unruly than elderly white women. If a thousand young black men were to come up and punch us in the mouth, we'd think no worse of black people, black men, or even young black men. We'd baulk at being near young men in general. Refusing to be wary of someone by race, we'd never look so easily at young white men again.

Certain there are no links between race (or culture) and the risk of bad behaviour, what remains is an abundance of other features we consider relevant to describing criminals. The clothes criminals wear while committing crimes or in court can make reports more interesting to read, as can their suburbs of residence and descriptions of their heights, weights, and small scars on their cheeks.

Strangely enough, words of detail include nationality of any Western country. Being an immigrant is only irrelevant to our descriptions of criminals who've immigrated from outside the West. The *Adelaide Now* website introduced Jason Downie, who in 2011 confessed to murdering the Rowe family in Kapunda, South Australia, with the description "*Scottish immigrant.*" The report made more of him being Scottish than it did of him growing up without a father since he was two months old.

Conversely, Australian Asians arrested on drug charges in Asia are simply Australians, even if they and their friends never describe themselves as such. They might even be the affectionate "Aussies," indistinguishable from the bronzed lifesavers on Bondi Beach.

When Robert El-Chammas twice raped an old woman in a park in May 2008, the *Topix* website reported his crime as 'Aussie Boy Raped 82 year old Korean Twice!' Whether El-Chammas was Australian born or even an Australian citizen was immaterial; living here meant every newspaper article I encountered described him as being Australian.

A response to the report was more informative. A person who knew him confirmed what his surname suggested, at least to anyone so racist as to wonder. Racially, he was Lebanese.

Another respondent, Dee, objected to the rape being used to defame Australians. She wrote that El-Chammas wasn't an Australian name.

A reader using the moniker "*Anglo Trash*" was furious, but not at the rapist. "*You ignorant moron with a cupp-cake "Irish" husband,*" he or she told Dee. "*LOL. What is an a Australian NAME? You ignorant racist dolt, the Anglo-Convicts have English names LOL. Only the Anglo-trash commit these crimes because the immigrants are to busy working and feeding you worthless boozy racist dole bludgers humping their own kin. LOL. You qualify for a PhD in IGNORANCE. You indeed are a sad pathetic racist basketcase. "Australian name" ...ROFLMAO..."*

Anglo Trash appeared to be Canadian, at least by residence, with no qualms about abusing the English as we don't dare defame other races. *"Almost all these sickos who commit deviant crimes in the penal colony are Anglo trash whose have no respect for others as they come from uneducated, racist, drunken broken incesteous families where grab an granny on a weekend is considered a date."*

Early in the 1990s, the only foreign nationality with a statistically higher rate of criminal behaviour than Australians in Australia was New Zealand, according to my local federal parliamentarian at the time, Philip Ruddock. He was arguing against race playing a role in immigration, but would never distinguish white New Zealanders from the Maoris and other Pacific Islanders. His was a statement about nationality, not race. Yet, any alleged lack of statistically significant links between nationality and criminality hasn't made nationality irrelevant to describing Western criminals not from New Zealand.

Identifying criminals' residency or nationality can be more problematic for countries where nationality connotes a race. We can still get it wrong.

A 2012 *Yahoo! News* headline spoke of a 'German girl locked up for years by Bosnian couple.' The German girl had been held for eight years, fed pumpkin and corn grain used to feed pigs, forced to pull a horse cart in place of the horse while her abductors sat in it laughing, tortured, and subjected to sexual abuse. I assumed the abductors were racially Bosnian, or at least Balkan. They weren't. They were gypsies.

There's a game around the races of criminals, for anyone willing to play. More fun than reading reports is deciphering them.

Naturally, news stories of a man charged with hiding a video camera in a shopping basket and filming up the skirts of female customers in a Sydney city supermarket, the third Thursday night in March 2012, made no mention of his race. Investigators interviewing him required the aid of a Korean interpreter.

Race is irrelevant to our descriptions of criminals. Language isn't.

Plasterer Mustafa Kunduraci murdered Greg Tucker and Korinne Aylward in December 2013, stabbing him eighteen times and her nine times in their Moonee Ponds home because they'd not paid him the money he wanted for defective renovations work. The couple's three children, aged between one and five years old, slept nearby. The only clue to Kunduraci's race (aside from his name) was a single reference to a Turkish interpreter assisting him at the initial court hearing.

I'm surprised that news reports regard the legal representation of an alleged criminal as being relevant, given what it can reveal. Parolee Roderick Holohan assaulted and attempted to rob a woman at Kings Cross the second Wednesday of May 2009. Six hours later, he violently assaulted and robbed a policewoman walking through Rushcutters Bay Park. He seemed white in the clouded version of his face appearing in news photographs after his arrest, when the Aboriginal Legal Service represented him.

The Aboriginal Legal Service seems to get a lot of work defending clients accused of crime. The crimes aren't corporate fraud or embezzlement.

Jobs are relevant to our descriptions of criminals. Paul Wilkinson promised his pregnant mistress, nurse Kylie Labouchardiere (whose father had served in the Australian Army for twenty-five years), he would leave his wife and set up home with her in Dubbo, but to keep his marriage intact, he murdered her. For no particular reason, I assumed Wilkinson was white throughout the news reports providing an abundance of details about the trial and its characters, until one mentioned his past job. Being a former New South Wales police officer didn't imply anything about his race. Being a former Aboriginal liaison officer did.

Receiving government welfare payments is always relevant, much as a job would be, for its financial implications. One of two people charged in Melbourne Magistrates Court with a forty-four million dollar drug haul the second Thursday of July 2011 was a mother (of two teenage children) receiving welfare. There was no mention of race, but with names like Thi Truong Tran and Manh Dao we could guess.

Being a parent is also relevant to our descriptions of criminals. A 2012 headline in the *Sydney Morning Herald* newspaper spoke of a "*hard-working family man*" who'd paid ten dollars to girls aged from twelve to fourteen years old to perform sexual acts on him. He was Elia Toma, who'd immigrated from Iraq thirty-two years earlier.

Even bicycles are relevant. What were called simply three youths riding bicycles chased two Sri Lankan youths into the Stockwell Food and Wine Shop in Brixton, south London the last Tuesday in March 2011. They stopped at the door and fired their guns indiscriminately, shooting a five-year-old girl in the chest and a shopkeeper in the head. Barny Stutter, an owner of nearby Brixton Cycles, described the people regularly hassling workers in the area's fast-food shops merely as yobs. "The truth is, the gunman's probably about fifteen with a mentality of about five."

Age is a point of description and denigration. Race isn't, although it was hard to imagine anyone in Brixton being British.

"Young people are such cowards," said Jono the tiler in our home the first Wednesday morning in April 2010, responding to news reports of four boys punching Scottish tourist Mark Willis, knocking him to the footpath, and leaving him fighting for his life. (Australians knew not to be out so early in the morning in Rockdale.)

Jono and I said nothing more, although I confess I'd worked enough on this writing to wonder what race the assailants were. Deep down in the first news reports, when police were still searching for suspects, two were described as having "*dark complexion*" and two "*medium complexion*." All had black hair.

When they were arrested, all mention of their skin and hair colours vanished. Two became "*twin schoolboys*," aged thirteen. All four were too young for their names to be reported. Without white pangs about racism, they'd taunted Willis for his Scottish accent.

Race isn't relevant, relatives are. News reports of the conviction of Michael El Ali and Houssam Khaled El Ali from Katoomba for twenty child sex offences, including rape, and the supply of drugs, didn't mention their race. They mentioned them being brothers.

A news report that Omar Artan sexually assaulted a fourteen-year-old girl in Preston, Victoria, in October 2009 didn't mention his race. It did mention he was nephew to former Somali dictator Mohammed Siad Barre. Married in January after the assault, Artan's two-year gaol sentence was wholly suspended for two years because Judge Roy Punshon believed he felt shamed by the sexual assault, had pleaded guilty, and had previously been of good character. That made it all right.

Race is irrelevant to violent behaviour. Music isn't.

John Ratzenberger played the wonderfully serious fool Cliff

Clavin in the television comedy series *Cheers*. In 2009, he sought a restraining order against his former girlfriend. The legal papers he filed with the Los Angeles County Superior Court claimed she'd *"indicated that it is common in many country western songs for women to set the cars of their former boyfriends on fire. That statement insinuates that she may have the capacity to perpetuate this act or similar violent conduct."* Clavin, sorry Ratzenberger, thus alleged she'd implied she was capable of violence against him because she listened to country western music.

15. WEAPONRY

I only learnt that London had suffered race riots as long ago as 1958 in a newspaper article that mentioned the background to West Indians starting the Notting Hill Carnival in 1966. Police arrested more than hundred people on the first day of the 2016 carnival, one quarter of them for carrying bladed weapons. The next day, three children and a twenty-year-old man were stabbed at the Children's Day Parade.

"I think by nature we are born racist," said Bernard Makeny, a Sudanese immigrant to Australia, in 2008, not referring only to Sudanese. "As a civilised society we have to limit it, to develop a positive attitude." Whether he would have spoken in such terms before coming to Australia in 2001, I don't know. Conflict between Africans and Arabs in Darfur had killed half a million people through violence and disease in the five years since 2003. (Racially homogeneous societies presumably don't need to limit their racist natures.)

Makeny seemed to acknowledge that white people formed racial stereotypes from negative experiences or other sordid reality, which he thought we should ignore. He'd written two short films, *The Applicant* and *Colour Blind*, to improve Australians' opinions about African immigrants.

He wasn't contemplating Sudanese forming positive attitudes about us. Then again, neither do we.

In our Western vision of the world, Africans don't kill. Knives, alcohol, and males do.

Soon after midnight one Monday morning in April 2008, a group of Africans on Granville railway station asked a Fijian, Eddie Spowart, for a cigarette. Spowart didn't smoke and so couldn't give them one. Thus, they murdered him. *"Police are appealing for anyone who may have witnessed the incident or noticed a group of black African males in the vicinity of Granville Railway Station, Memorial Avenue or near the bus interchange on Mary Street around 12.45am yesterday, to contact Rosehill Police or Crime Stoppers..."*

Two years passed before I read anything more about it, below a headline identifying the killer only as a fifteen-year-old boy. The "cowardly and vengeful" murder "demonstrates yet again the havoc that is wreaked all too often when a knife is carried in public by intoxicated males," said Judge Megan Latham, "who resort to violence to vindicate themselves over some relatively petty slight."

Being a Sudanese refugee only mitigated culpability. "It might be said that his exposure to violence in the Sudan and Kenya desensitised him to some extent to the use of violence in order to settle disputes," said the sympathetic judge.

Working with several youth charities taught musician Angry Anderson that Australians normally fought with their fists, but Lebanese, Indochinese, and Pacific Islanders used deadly weapons. "The racial thing, the cultural thing needs to be addressed because it's not going to go away," he told an Australian parliamentary inquiry into youth violence early in 2010. "Aussie kids didn't use weapons," repeated Anderson outside Parliament House, of the era before the 1980s. Insisting he wasn't racist, he said we needed to deal with racial difference. "We've got to tell Lebanese kids and Indochinese kids that it might be all right where you come from, but it's not all right here."

I'd thought we'd already done that, unless we'd forgotten to mention it. Perhaps we felt saying so would have been unwelcoming.

Anti-Discrimination Board president Stepan Kerkyasharian immediately rebuked him. "To suggest that if people of a particular kind of culture weren't here a particular kind of violence wouldn't occur is pure fantasy," he insisted, without Anderson's practical experience but his politics clear. His words were untrue.

Race Discrimination Commissioner Graham Innes agreed with Anderson that "some violence in Australia has a racial aspect," and had since the goldfields in the nineteenth century. (We should have learned to accept it.) "Violence amongst racial groups is not new," he said, not letting criticism of other races go by without making the same criticism of his. "The white settlers were violent towards Aboriginal people."

Innes never explained what that violence was, but we assume it. We talk of violence by Europeans against Aborigines more than two hundred years ago as we don't talk about violence by other races ever. "We need a zero-tolerance policy from government," said Innes, as if policies can deal with all our problems, "to say that multicultural violence is not tolerated."

I didn't understand what multicultural violence meant. Perhaps Innes wanted violence kept within a race.

I recalled Anderson's words when I read a newspaper article of a mass brawl on the second floor of a restaurant on Beamish Street, Campsie one evening in September 2010. More than thirty Asian men brawling mightn't have been news, except two were slashed with knives. They walked to Canterbury Hospital for treatment, while the other men left the restaurant.

All the brawlers were Asian. It thus wasn't multicultural violence.

Early the summer evening three days after Christmas 2010, on the busy foreshore a hundred metres from the St Kilda Sea Baths in Melbourne, up to ten men carrying weapons broke into an altercation with five teenage skateboarders. The men smashed a skateboarder with a bottle, causing his head and forearm to bleed badly, and stabbed him many times over with a meat cleaver. "One of the skater guys was screaming: 'Get an ambulance'," said James McMorrow sitting in a park nearby. "We went over there, and the skater was lying on the ground and blood was all over his face. His leg was twitching."

From the newspaper photograph, all the skateboarders were white. Only because the assailants had fled and police were looking for them could we learn they were Asian. That must have been multicultural violence.

During the 1990s, I heard a speaker on the radio refute the suggestion that Asians were more criminal than Australians by attributing Asians' heavier sentences and incarceration rates to their greater propensity to use knives. Our institutional white racism was the criminal justice system's insensitivity to knives.

Asians weren't the only immigrants keen to use knives. My childhood neighbour Bruce finished Normanhurst Boys' High School in 1981. More than three decades later, he mentioned the day a mob of Lebanese arrived at the school with knives because somebody had slighted a Lebanese student. At the time, with all he was being told in school, he didn't link the incident with them being Lebanese. I don't recall hearing about it then.

One day the third week of November 2010, my eldest daughter's high school was in lockdown. That Saturday, another father told me that a boy's father and brothers had come to the school to attack a boy with whom he'd been fighting the previous day. Knowing we individually minded white people don't fight for our families (which worked well when our countries were racially homogenous), I suggested, "It sounds like the Lebanese."

He didn't know. I think he was the man who told me of a Puerto Rican boy with him at Dulwich Hill High School in the 1970s. A rare interracial immigrant in Australia then, fighting with another boy in a tuckshop line, he revealed his fist to have wire wrapped around it. He slashed the other boy's face. (Knives seemed relatively harmless.)

Harmony Day celebrations in 2011 would've been particularly interesting at Granville Boys High School. The school was in lockdown the last Wednesday of February after a fifteen-year-old boy stabbed another boy five times in the playground. There was no mention of race, but one distressed mother rushing to the school afterwards, checking upon the well-being of her son, was Rawa. He wasn't involved.

"It's a schoolyard fight where someone has produced a weapon," said Granville police inspector Garry Sims, playing down the stabbing. "There's no culture of weapons and violence in the school."

He lied. Three or four years earlier, a race-hating film emerged from students at the school. A group of them stormed a nearby school with machetes and baseball bats.

In the first term of 2010, forty-two assaults in public schools in western and south-western Sydney were reported to the School Safety and Response Unit of the Education Department. There were thirty-four reports for weapons in the same area, accounting for almost half of all weapons found in New South Wales schools.

Bassam Saddik, a youth worker with the Granville Youth Association, saw the students carrying weapons more as victims than assailants. "People who feel unprotected, who don't feel safe, might feel like they have to carry a weapon," he said. "Whether it be Granville Boys or private, posher schools, people carry weapons to school, carry drugs to school."

He didn't specify those private, posher schools, but no boys brought weapons to mine. Nor did he speak to race or religion.

Young people banding together under a "gang" name was no different from playground antics involving "cool" groups or "nerds," claimed Saddik. "A lot of these guys feel they need to belong to an organisation or a group," he said. "It doesn't necessarily have to be a bad thing." Weaponry and gang activity were insignificant. "You're always going to get one idiot, one boof head…and that person just ruins the whole day for everyone." (It certainly ruined the day for the boy stabbed five times.)

When we're around other races not shy to use weapons, we can't remain oblivious to weaponry as we remain oblivious to race. Multiculturalism compels some people take up arms they otherwise wouldn't.

There was thus a rare reference to Asian gangs in a 2012 report in the *Age* newspaper, although the report wasn't about gangs. It was about a white woman breaking the law.

Natasha Adams had appeared before a Melbourne court for having made a false customs declaration at Tullamarine airport the previous year. As well as her father collecting martial arts items, she told Judge Mark Dean that she and her brother needed items she hadn't declared in her customs form because they lived in Springvale, where there were a "lot of Asian gangs." Her luggage had been found to contain an electric shock device in the form of a mobile telephone, three extendable batons, four flick knives, three knuckledusters, and a throwing star.

They're weapons for people without guns. Other people have guns.

Through the neighbourhood watch scheme, I receive police briefing sheets sent to local media. Without mentioning people's names or races, only their ages and genders, they list significant motor vehicle crashes, drunk driving, shoplifting, and vandalism. Police had much to say about the signs stolen from Turramurra High School late in 2008, but never mentioned the act of a student with my eldest son in year seven at our local high school the third Monday of October. Leo, who was Chinese or possibly Korean, brought bullets to school.

Two days later, among the pupils waiting on the railway station nearest the school, a year-eight student pushed my son from the platform towards the path of a coming train. My son wasn't hurt. The student, Wayne, was Chinese or possibly Korean. At least there were no weapons involved, aside from the train.

Grandfather Bob Knight liked to dress up as Santa Claus for children at Christmas time. A perfectionist in his work, he was driving his truck through Milperra the last Thursday of June 2009 when a stray bullet from a gunfight several streets away struck him. He managed to swerve the truck to stop safely in the traffic before he died. The *Daily Telegraph* newspaper called the killing a *"KFC gunfight,"* for the fast-food restaurant where the shootout occurred. Deep down, the report mentioned Moustapha Mahmoud being involved in the shooting and his brother Mariam fleeing police. It was the irrelevance of race, but relevance of chicken.

Blaming not the brothers nor multiculturalism, the innocent truck driver's death was more of the bad luck to which we attribute crime in our multicultural West. The *Sydney Morning Herald* newspaper called it *"random madness."*

The second Tuesday in March 2012, New South Wales police (including the Middle Eastern crime squad) raided eleven properties in Sydney. At Sylvania Waters post office, they seized a parcel containing a hundred and forty Glock pistol magazines, seven firearms, ammunition, drugs, and computer equipment. Police charged a post office licensee, a worker at an import business, and a telecommunications technician with *"a raft of offences including supplying firearms, aggravated possession of firearms and participating in a criminal group."*

German police also arrested a man in Remscheid. Crime is global, at least through the West. We call it freedom of movement, freedom of trade.

"We will be alleging these guns were being imported specifically for use by criminals," said police commissioner Andrew Scipione, "including outlaw motorcycle gang members and those in Middle Eastern organised crime groups." It was a terrible slander on motorcycle gangs.

Never are we more blasé about crime than when criminals are content killing their own. 'Another night, another drive-by shooting as Sydney house targeted,' said a *Sydney Morning Herald* headline in August 2011. Two nights earlier, shots were fired into a house on Eddy Street, Merrylands West, where Mouhamed and Sleiman Tajjour used to live. The second shooting was into two cars parked outside a house in Lachlan Street, Bossley Park and into the garage. Another shooting that night in Barcom Street, Merrylands left two men in hospital, although police believed that followed a broken relationship.

Over the ensuing weeks and months, the shootings continued,

night after night. By early 2012, Sydney was starting to fret. None of the victims were saying anything to police. No news reports referred to anyone's race or religion, but people willing to contemplate thought the shooters and targets were Arabs. The *Sydney Morning Herald* responded by reporting a random drive-by shooting with the victim's name, Albert Slater, from 1929, along with shootings in 1936, two in 1937, and 1938. We were supposed to see that crime with guns was nothing new and wasn't peculiar to Arabs.

Former New South Wales assistant police commissioner Clive Small recognised differences between past shootings and present-day shootings, beyond merely their frequency. "Middle Eastern crime figures saw that there were opportunities that they could use to get to the top," he said in 2011, referring to the Wood Royal Commission into police corruption a decade earlier. "These were drive-by shootings that were mixed in with straight-out murder, kidnapping, or kneecappings… What you also have to remember, is that many of these victims of drive-by shootings are not innocent victims. They know what the shooting is about." The shootings continued.

None of it quite compared with our multicultural model, Sweden, with her policies we consider enlightened. By the summer of 2015, Malmö was being rocked by hand grenade attacks, among more than thirty explosions until September that year, up from twenty-five in 2014. Bomb disposal units assigned to Malmö described it as being eerily similar to the Middle East in which they'd worked.

Immigration eventually transforms our countries into the countries from which the immigrants come. They're the reason those countries are like that.

16. MARKETING MULTICULTURALISM

A great failing of governments is their unwillingness to admit their mistakes. That used to make democracies beneficial for the chance to change governments and so policies. They no longer are.

During a visit to democratic America in the 1980s, the last leader of the communist Soviet Union, Mikhail Gorbachev, observed that the communist dictatorship's media control never achieved the uniformity of propaganda that free America had. He'd have interpreted that blanket ideology as capitalism, but it's individualism through all its devolving forms, including multiculturalism. Our proudly empowered free public insists we don't trust journalists. We still wind up believing them.

We persist with interracial immigration in spite of its appalling record, certain we're succeeding. The multiracial West founded upon ideology and naïvety is sustained by marketing and spin. Without them, there'd be all sorts of dissent.

Questioning multiculturalism because of particular individuals might seem spurious, but we tirelessly tout the benefits of immigration by citing individuals. Success makes their race relevant, as it's not for successful white people.

Foremost among them through the 1980s was surgeon Victor Chang, born in Shanghai to Australian-born Chinese parents. We talked of his presence being a benefit, losing our sense that white people can achieve what immigrants achieve. Chang might have pioneered heart transplants wherever he lived. An Australian would've done so had Chang not lived in Australia.

We didn't speak of Malaysians Chiew Seng Liew and Phillip Choon Tee Lim being a burden. The first Thursday morning in July 1991, they tried to kidnap Chang from his Mercedes Benz driving to work along a normally serene Mosman street. When he refused to enter their car, they murdered him.

While refusing to generalise the bad deeds by individuals of other races to the rest of those races, we generalise the good. We generalise not the criminals of other races, but the victims.

Refugee advocate Julian Burnside didn't just trust without question Afghan refugee Najaf Mazari, who claimed in his 2008 book *The Rugmaker of Mazar-e-Sharif* to have suffered injustice while loving people so much. Burnside insisted the book's *"importance and its power lies in the fact that it is the story of all refugees."* It plainly was not.

Race is always relevant to stories of how good other races are. In 2014, the South Australian government recommended Her Majesty the Queen appoint Hieu Van Le the state's next governor. In response, my friend Sonia cited Rob M on her Facebook computer page to say that, had the Australian government in 1977 kept out Vietnamese refugees coming by boat, then South Australia would have had no governor at the end of 2014, as if Australia's entire system of government would have collapsed without refugees.

"Not really, Sonia," I thought of typing. *"South Australia might just have had a South Australian governor."* Sonia never responded to refugee crime by saying that, had the government kept out refugees, somebody wouldn't have been robbed, raped, or killed.

The third Thursday in February 2015, my second son's year-eight geography teacher told the class that the coming of refugees was a benefit of immigration. My son pointed out that the Iranian cleric who'd held seventeen people hostage at the Lindt Café two months earlier, at the end of which two hostages died, had been a refugee. The teacher accused him of calling all refugees terrorists. She said a white person could have committed the crime, to which my son pointed out that a white person hadn't. She asked if he was calling her a terrorist for being a refugee from Italy. (I can't think of any refugees we've ever accepted from Italy.)

We generalise all immigrants to be like the best of them. We assume anyone who doesn't is generalising them all to be like the worst of them.

His geography teacher concluded by saying my son had been indoctrinated by the media, but the media had been very coy in reporting the Lindt Café siege. In spite of Man Haron Monis demanding hostages hold an Islamic flag in Arabic against the café windows, the Australian Broadcasting Corporation television coverage went for something like seven hours before mentioning Islam. Presumably the media shouldn't have reported the sixteen-hour siege in busy Martin Place at all.

The Australian government responded to the Lindt Café siege

by announcing it would spend more than half a billion dollars teaching immigrants Australian values and the English language. It reflected our confidence we could create multicultural harmony by expending enough money and with enough education, but eighteen years in Australia and learning English had only made Monis angrier at the country that gave him refuge and money.

(Our refusal to link race or culture to crime means we don't consider increased policing, security, surveillance, and intelligence costs in the economics of immigration. Some races and cultures increase those costs more than others; we never expended vast sums of money and effort trying to keep European immigrants from becoming criminals and terrorists.)

Marketing racial diversity makes immigrant success stories important to tell. They can't help but make people want to throw open all borders to everyone wanting to come.

The *Sydney Morning Herald* newspaper dedicated a long article in 2008 to the smiling Bedraie family also from Iran, with a charming colour photograph. Tales of the trauma they said they'd suffered and horrors they said they'd witnessed in mandatory detention gave way to stories of the father's small painting business, mother's work in childcare, and son's love of soccer settled into their wonderful new life in the western suburbs of Sydney. Far from the *Herald*'s primary readership in the affluent northern and eastern suburbs, they were never likely to meet.

Conversely, that same edition of the newspaper devoted about a third as many words to German police removing two suspected terrorists from a Dutch aeroplane at Bonn-Cologne airport. Speaking of citizenship not race, one was a Somali and the other a German, born in Somalia. There were no pictures, no stories to tell.

I don't know whether the tale of the Bedraie family was true. The cleverest propaganda is. Similar articles about the pains and joys of people murdered, raped, or even accidentally harmed or killed by immigrants don't appear in newspapers. Propaganda becomes the stories untold.

In November 2010, twenty-nine miners, including two Australians, were trapped in the Pike River Mine in New Zealand. Days of hope the men might've been alive ended with explosions that meant they were dead. The drama and tragedy attracted extensive news coverage in Australia (although I only learnt the following September that environmental constraints had prevented the mine from having been made safer).

Attracting ever more coverage a month later were the deaths of thirty Iraqis, Kurds, and Iranians sneaking into Australia to claim refugee status when their boat crashed on Christmas Island. A journalist for the *Crikey* website called it "*a national tragedy.*"

News media reported details of lost lives as we'd never read of the miners. Iraqi asylum seeker Madian El Ibrahimy was "*OVERWHELMED with grief*" (the capital letters not mine) and collapsed after his family died.

"I can't eat," said his older brother Oday, living in Auburn, who wanted him released to his care. "I can't sleep. Two days, no eating nothing, I'm not sleeping. I'm worried about my brother." He said he'd undertaken the same dangerous journey from the Shi'ite holy city of Najaf his brother and aunt had taken eight years earlier, after their father and other relatives were executed by Saddam Hussein's regime.

I couldn't help but wonder if any of it was true. Truth wouldn't have made any difference.

Gone are the days that journalist Philip Adams (I think it was) criticised the West for making more of the death of one of our own than of anyone else. Promoting immigration, we make more of the deaths of other races. There are deaths and relative deaths, according to whether the relatives are ours.

Reports of kind refugees aren't ambivalent. They're euphoric.

The story of Bolis Longy and his wife Awatif Shomoo did more than mention they were Sudanese refugees. It defined them as such in the headline. A well-educated father of five unable to find a job and turning to farming would probably not be reported were he white. It certainly wouldn't be written with such asides as his three-year-old twins being "*cute as buttons.*" (We have no pretence of objectivity when complimenting other races.)

The Department of Immigration and Citizenship hadn't merely accepted them as refugees. It contributed funds to the African Food Project, giving them small plot farms in Australia. If that seemed unduly generous, then the article talked of the persecution Longy and his family had supposedly suffered in the Sudan. To assuage us still further, it mentioned Longy being a volunteer minister at his local Baptist church and writing a book in Arabic about Christian values.

Christianity is never more fondly described than in articles about refugees. An article about Sudanese refugee Mach Maluak (hoping to get a job), his wife, and three children spoke of them being Christian.

We market immigration by claiming immigrants help us. We market asylum by claiming refugees suffered, much as they do.

Being failed asylum seekers was at the forefront of five contestants on the Dutch television game show *Weg van Nederland* in 2011. Deportees were never less menacing and never more attractive than an aeronautical engineer facing return to Cameroon or a Slavic languages student headed back to Chechnya, talking about Dutch culture as if it were theirs. "We're hoping *Weg van Nederland* makes more people think about how we treat asylum seekers," explained Wouter van Zandwijk from asylum seeker advocacy group *Vluchtelingenwerk*, "that they understand what asylum seekers go through."

My eldest son's geography teacher showed his class the Australian Broadcasting Corporation television propaganda piece *Go Back to Where You Came From*. Very cleverly, the programme picked people concerned about refugees coming to Australia and subjected them to a journey like one refugees claimed to have taken, up to a point. (There was no chance of a television series called *Thanks for Coming*, when refugee advocates meet people assaulted by refugees and families of people murdered by refugees.)

We taint the news of other races. We taint their skin colours, too.

Among the few places in Europe I haven't visited is Kosovo. When Western countries began accepting Muslim Kosovars fleeing Serbia in the 1990s, television images broadcast their apparently white faces. Being a good, postmodern German and Christian, neither their race nor religion dissuaded my friend Bruce's wife Edith from helping them. She told me their complexions were swarthy. News services presumably falsified their faces to cajole Western opinion.

Many years later, a news item inadvertently corroborated Edith's words. On New Year's Eve 2008, a swarthy-faced gunman with dark hair and a dark moustache murdered two Israelis in a crowded Copenhagen shopping mall, following Israeli retaliation for Palestinian rocket attacks in the Gaza strip. Speculation centred on the national origins (and, dare we say, race) of the gunman. "We cannot say whether he is Palestinian, Iraqi, Iranian, or Bosnian or where he is from," said a police spokesman.

The gunman proved to be Palestinian. News services reported his arrest as *"Danish man arrested over mall shooting."*

A year later, New Year's Eve 2009, a gunman killed his Finnish former girlfriend in her home before killing four of her colleagues in a shopping mall in the Helsinki suburb of Espoo. A father of three formerly married to a Kosovar, he was Ibrahim Shkupolli from Kosovo. He'd been living in Finland since 1990.

We expect politicians and journalists not to mention immigrant crimes, at least as *their* crimes, for fear of stoking prejudice against them. *"Thanks Colin Barnett and News Limited for stirring up the rascist, bogan, redneck scum of Australia,"* complained Dog Whistle of Bogan Island, after the West Australian premier said the Australian government shouldn't release forty Afghan asylum seekers into the community because one or more of them deliberately set fire to their boat on Ashmore Reef. *"Some of you people make me sick. Pull your heads in and try to be a little generous to fellow humans in suffering for a change."* (Dog Whistle clearly had no generosity for fellow Australians.)

Kind to immigrants and seemingly free from prejudice was a young mother leaving the Star Bar nightclub in Bendigo at two o'clock in the morning, the second Sunday in January 2011. A sixteen-year-old girl introduced her to seven former refugees from Sudan and Afghanistan, aged from fourteen to twenty-one. The young mother invited them to her home, joining a babysitter charged with looking after her children.

While those children slept nearby, their party was pleasant, until Aru Gar placed his arms around the young mother. With his mobile telephone, another man recorded her being grabbed in the kitchen while a sixteen-year-old boy tried dragging her into the laundry. "No," she kept saying, while he and a fourteen-year-old boy kept trying to shepherd her into the laundry. She continually pushed them away, but Gar lifted her skirt and pulled down her underwear. The other men and boys laughed, while she screamed and he digitally raped her.

The men took her into the laundry where Mohammed El Nour and the sixteen-year-old held her down. For half an hour she was there, screaming, while Akoak Manon and a seventeen-year-old raped her. The sixteen-year-old slapped her and digitally raped her.

Normally, refugee status and race disappear when refugees

commit crimes. Initial news reports spoke only of a past boyfriend murdering model and university student Sammi Hewitt in Hobart the weekend before Harmony Day 2011 and then killing himself. Being Tasmania, I'd assumed the killer was also Australian, until I saw a photograph of Kuol Piom.

Murders were still uncommon in Tasmania, but so were Sudanese. A later headline was more explicit, identifying readers with not the victim but the suicidal murderer. 'Tasmania's Sudanese community is struggling to come to grips with the death of one of its own.'

"No one thought he could do that," said Sudanese executive committee member Owak Awak. "He was a very outgoing person, very social person, who was kind and loving and he loved Sammi."

Sudanese were more shocked for Piom's death than his victim's. So were we.

According to the *Mercury* newspaper, Piom left a Uganda refugee camp in 2007 and *"made a successful life since moving to Australia as a youngster and becoming an Australian citizen."* He'd *"adjusted to life in Australia well, particularly since moving closer to his family in Tasmania about two years ago. Mr Piom had many friends, he said, and played basketball for the Breakers Basketball Club and also assisted with Tasmania's national basketball team, the Hobart Chargers."* I'm not sure I'd ever before read of a murderer being described in such glowing terms.

"Mr Awak said his cousin was not a bad man. However, he now feared the Sudanese community would receive unwarranted retribution because of Mr Piom's actions. 'When incidents happen we get stigmatised,' he said. 'We are not bad people, we are Australian people, just like everyone else. We are a kind community, one big family, and we are struggling with this just as much as others.'"

It was easy to forget Piom had murdered his former girlfriend. The news report cared more about him killing himself. *"People seeking support and information about suicide prevention can call Lifeline on 131 114."*

17. MULTICULTURAL CITIES

My youngest daughter's poster for the local historical society's fiftieth-anniversary writing competition can only have benefited from mentioning Harmony Day. She was a joint winner, as we all are.

Two things were interesting about the fortieth anniversary of the start of the American children's television show *Sesame Street*, in November 2009. One was that it warranted far more attention than the twentieth anniversary of the fall of the Berlin Wall: the most obvious expression of the collapse of Soviet communism.

The other, Brother Ned Gerber told me at dinner after church. "When it started," he said, "*Sesame Street* began with an image of an inner-city slum with ruined cars and garbage cans. It was to help children from those places relate to the show. Now, it's all bright flowers. It seems a sort of political correctness not to show those things."

I shook my head. "No matter how hard you could try to imagine something crazy about our society," I replied, "you just can't come up with anything more bizarre than the reality. There's whole parts of our cities, whole suburbs, that people just don't go to, and we have this blindness that they even exist."

Sesame Street was filmed in New York, which didn't mean the slum had necessarily been in New York any more than the flowers were. While cities deteriorated, our impressions of them blossomed: our urban illusion. We believe the publicity.

Robert Huber could have been describing much of the West in his article 'Being White in Philly: Whites, race, class, and the things that never get said,' for *Philadelphia* magazine in March 2013. "*I've begun to think that most white people stopped looking around at large segments of our city,*" he wrote, "*at our poorest and most dangerous neighborhoods, a long time ago. One of the reasons, plainly put, is queasiness over race. Many of those neighborhoods are predominantly African-American. And if you're white, you don't merely avoid them—you do your best to erase them from your thoughts.*" Realities seemingly inescapable, we escape.

Calling the tone of the article "disgusting," the mayor Michael Nutter promptly asked the Human Relations Commission to examine the article's racial aspects. The proportion of white people living in Philadelphia had fallen from eighty percent in 1950 to thirty-seven percent.

Facts about race become a little like sitting in a chair in a pathologist's clinic, when the pending pain can make life seem awful. Rather than looking down at my tender arm and skin where shortly a needle will drain blood, I see the walls, carpet, and words on a poster behind the door. Like lying in a dentist's chair, feeling breath through my lungs, a looming drill can make me wish my life skipped that long minute or two. The time will come when I'm old and infirm looking back longingly to those days, for all their drills and needles, fearful of any dose of reality.

At their worst, cities and parts of cities grand only a generation or two earlier lie practically in ruin. Vast tracts of America's inner cities are unrecognisable from their images in old films, most obviously Los Angeles, New York, and St Louis. They're not settings so often for films anymore, except at the extremes that make them distant, comic book fantasies, like the surfaces of other planets. Their undefined squalor makes reality around us seem better. All I've heard or seen of Gary, Indiana are photographs of decay: a previously impressive stone railway station with broken windows and rotting walls.

We live our heady days of splendour in the suburbs, where conversations rarely turn to shadow streets. They get little mention in our evening news, except as stories of renewal each time a park is laid. Rather than risk linking their degeneration with the coming of other races, we blame governments failing to provide infrastructure, as if a few more concrete pylons could make everything all right.

More often than not, we don't think of them at all. We lose them behind thick silver mirrors reflecting images of shopping malls we've seen. Our altogether-visions in television programmes and commercials are of sanitised streets and peaceful places, with happy people and good purchasing. We're not trying to improve them because we think our pretty cities can't get any better, unless chance befalls us. Among the people who left Sydney's North Shore to campaign for the Liberal Party candidate in an Auburn state by-election in 2001, Di returned exclaiming, "It's just like

Beirut!"

I'd previously been to Auburn, so had no need to exclaim. I'd never been to Beirut.

Rowe Street had been a lovely mall when Eastwood was Australian, but I'd not been there for more than fifteen years when I returned in April 2013. Grubby and crass, in spite of the old fountain, Chinese commerce of anything at all jammed every store, spilling outside. By any standard but a complete rejection of everything Western and embracing of everything else, Rowe Street had markedly declined.

Standing outside the pharmacy in Rowe Street never used to be a security guard. A rare person there not East Asian, perhaps the pharmacists couldn't trust their own to defend them from their own. He was Middle Eastern.

We accept without question the security guards posted around shopping centres and in hospitals, government offices, and other public places. We're not cognisant of never having needed them before immigrants became so numerous.

At their best, our streets are simply dirtier. My first visit to London was with my father in 1979. His first and last trip there had been in 1953, but the city he recalled was clean. I couldn't have known had he not told me, but London had become conspicuously dirty since then. Contemporary reality bit back.

It's hard for us to know what life was like before we came of age, beyond the histories that teachers and books inform us and that films and television convince us. Older people telling us their olden-day memories could teach us the past, but we too rarely ask and even more rarely listen. Old people can be so negative.

We think our cities are clean because we compare them to the worst of the world's slums, unaware of what they were and might've remained, were they still ours. We know only of washrooms at petrol stations and railway stations being locked because of the risk of vandalism, opened by keys we borrow from attendants. They used to be unlocked.

Early in the 1990s, Australian Liberal Party leader John Hewson created a furore by publicly repeating a common adage that a visitor could always spot the tenanted houses in a street: the lawns were unmown, paths unswept, and gardens unkempt. Without any sense that something is ours, we have no reason to keep anything good or make anything better. In multiracial suburbs and cities, we're all tenants now. Without others keeping streets clean, we stopped bothering.

I enjoyed my time in bustling Istanbul, the summer of 1993, when the Turks had joy and self-confidence unlike Europeans, but the streets were dirty. When first I visited Denmark two years later, streets there were clean, not merely for being rich. Another year onward, Gothenburg, Sweden, was also clean, aside from the square about which black men mulled.

We don't let litter be reason not to welcome the newcomers. We employ street cleaners, who'd presumably not yet reached the Gothenburg square that Sunday morning.

Among the Western cities once impressive was Madrid, where I spent the weekend before Christmas, 1997. Walking that Sunday evening from the Palace Hotel to a restaurant as the hotel concierge said I could safely do, an arm thrust around my neck, pulling my head aback. A second youth grabbed my wallet. A third youth grabbed my camera bag, its strap around my neck.

Struggling to breathe, I tried to hold my chin down and forward to guard my throat. Choking with the arm locked at my throat, I said, "I'll give you the money."

One youth took my wallet. With another youth's arm around my neck, squeezing against it the strap of my camera bag, they could not take my camera bag. They ran away.

Walking towards me, on the other side of the street, was a well-dressed middle-aged apparently Spanish couple. "Did you see that?" I asked them. "I've been mugged." They ignored me.

I'd lost all my Spanish cash, although some pounds sterling and my airline tickets and passport were secure in another wallet at the hotel. If not the hotel concierge then a police officer (through a hotel employee translating) told me the youths who attacked me were Moroccan. Police knew of their crimes.

We reject talk of race and imagine everything being good, but our cities were gentler, more peaceful places when they were ours. Streets and suburbs where once we walked, even promenaded, conversing with strangers, we've become wary. It's hard not to contemplate there'd be less crime without the races we've allowed to share our countries, that we'd feel safer leaving our homes were our neighbourhoods still racially homogenous. We're the victims of crime and would be victims more often, but we're too scared to venture out at night and careful where we go by day.

18. BALKANISATION

Within Western countries, we were free to move around, for the most part. Through a developing series of judgments from *Brown v Board of Education of Topeka* in 1954 until *Swann v Charlotte-Mecklenburg Board of Education* in 1971, the American Supreme Court mandated moving around, busing, for Negroes in public school students. Pursuing racial equality in education, it demanded integration.

We also opened our countries to other races. We now close ourselves in small places, shut off from everyone else.

The first Wednesday of November 2007, I attended a cocktail party promoting a beachfront property development at Seven Mile Beach, near Forster, which Babcock & Brown developed with the curiously named Wise Property Group. Musicians played classical music, Aborigines danced. A slickly choreographed film promoted not a village but an array of private houses concealed from each other by trees and sealed from the world with a wall and the Booti Booti National Park. Boutique shops, gymnasiums, restaurants, cafés, and a "*hedonistic day spa*," meant that residents never needed to leave. "*This is the last great escape*," said the huge, colourful book given to all of us attending, "*a secret destination known only to a fortunate few.*"

We love being told our hidden homes are exclusive, if only to people rich enough to buy there. Seclusion is our isolation. Others can make harmony outside.

They don't. White construction worker Marty Marshall hadn't moved far in his career, but still America and freedom were something for him, his wife, and their two children to celebrate the last Saturday night of June 2009. They watched fireworks at the Firestone Stadium, Ohio, before gathering outside a friend's home in South Akron. Without words or warning, fifty or so young black men attacked Marshall's friend. When Marshall tried to help him, they attacked him too. His fifteen-year-old daughter tried to help, but they pushed her to the ground. His wife pushed their son into the bushes where he hid, while the black men kicked and punched the older men lying on the ground. "This is our world," they told them. "This is a black world!"

Those of us whose worlds are private clubs and gated communities disagree, politely of course. Marshall wasn't so snug, that night in South Akron. He spent five days concussed and bruised in the critical care unit of the Akron General Medical Centre. "This makes you think about your freedom," he said later. "In all reality, where is your freedom when you have this going on?" The police didn't rush to call the attack a hate crime.

The West giving up our collective territorial rights allows other races to assert them in our place. Balkanisation refers to the division of a country or region into unco-operative or even belligerent smaller countries or regions. The term was first applied to divisions by race and religion in the Balkan Peninsular under the Ottoman Empire. It came into more common use with the collapse of the Ottoman and Russian empires after World War I. It's applicable to anywhere multiracial.

Removing formal borders between races led to informal borders between them; structured segregation gave way to unstructured segregation. Free market demographics means other races stake out territories we dare not breach.

"I never feel safe in Bankstown," said one woman who didn't want to be named, after Bill Crews, a young detective in training from rural Australia, was shot dead the previous night in a drug raid in Cairds Avenue in 2010. He'd been part of the Middle Eastern Organised Crime Squad, although Philip Nguyen killed him. "There seems to be a lot of crime."

Gus said Bankstown was a safe suburb. The news report didn't mention his race.

Sixteen-year-old Brandon Faananu Siaa, also known as Brandon Nunu Asiata, was headed home from a Technical and Further Education College the last Wednesday in May 2011. Mosa Julius Mbele, a father, confronted him. "I run Bankstown," Mbele told him. "I own Bankstown."

Siaa, a Samoan, responded by calling Mbele a "nigger." The two waged verbal and physical assaults against each other over who and whose gang controlled the suburb. (The only thing certain was that white people no longer did.)

Two hours later, in front of his brothers, friends, and

commuters, Mbele again confronted Siaa, slapped him twice across the face, and pulled a large dagger from beneath his hooded jumper. Mbele stabbed Siaa in the heart so severely that the blade snapped off, killing him within minutes. Mbele's South African parents insisted their son wasn't violent.

In the euphemistic way we speak of criminals, both were already known to police. (They weren't known for volunteering with Neighbourhood Watch.)

"You're not in Australia now," young Australian-born Lebanese, Afghans, and Iraqis, known as Generation Jihad, told reporters Janet Fife-Yeomans and Simon Black of Bankstown in 2013. Born in Sydney, Milad bin Ahmad-Shah al-Ahmadzai, called himself an ethnic Pashtun from Afghanistan. He'd been arrested for threatening to slit the throat of an Australian Commonwealth officer.

Much as swallows mark spring each year, rioters torching cars mark New Years' Eve across what reporters Thierry Leveque and Nick Vinocur in 2010 called France's *"sensitive urban areas."* Readers such as Greg Buls pointed out that meant the Islamic neighbourhoods, home to North African immigrants and their children and grandchildren. Among the scores of news reports and headlines I read that 2011 New Year, as I normally read, only that one mentioned the torching.

Another reader, Abhinav, applauded the civil disobedience keeping the government in check. He didn't say from what, but presumably from policing immigrants.

Police know where not to go, or not to go alone. My father told me of American cities in the 1970s where police cars entered in pairs, because single police cars had disappeared. Tourists often don't know the excluded areas.

Waiting in line to pay for petrol at a Chevron station near Memorial Stadium, Baton Rouge, one Sunday night in May 2013 was a white man, who black man Donald Dickerson teased for his pink shirt. Foolishly, the white man defended his choice of clothes. Dickerson told him he was in the wrong neighbourhood and wasn't going to make it out again. Dickerson punched him, knocking him to the ground, before black man Devin Bessye joined in. The victim's wife rushed from their car to help him. Black woman Ashley Simmons knocked her unconscious, too. Their teenage daughter followed. She too was hit unconscious.

The three assailants were already known to police, who charged Dickerson with battery. Exercising their discretion, police didn't charge the other two because they'd not sufficiently injured their victims. Nor did the police treat the assaults as racially motivated.

It still staggers me that people accuse Western police of prejudice against blacks. Perhaps Baton Rouge police should have also let Dickerson go.

The last Saturday afternoon before Christmas 1998, I was in Baltimore. The Poe House and Museum was closed on weekends, but I wanted to see its exterior. Soon enough, walking towards it, all the people around me were black.

A black man, perhaps about my age and carrying a sports bag, began walking with me. "Some of these people are dangerous," he told me. "I'll look after you."

My voice I kept modest, ordinary, ignorant of America, and sympathetic to everything he said. "Thanks for showing me the way," I said to him, after we reached the Poe House. "I guess I better get back to my hotel."

"It isn't safe," he said. "I'll protect you."

He said he wanted money, before he moved a little into my way. The open bag in his hand revealed a screwdriver he could plant in my skull. I gave him most of the money I carried.

I didn't bother reporting a crime to the police or making an insurance claim. Being a good white person, I blamed myself.

We blame circumstance for crime. We blame ourselves. We don't blame race or racial diversity.

We accept whole streets, suburbs, and even cities we can no longer so much as enter for our race. "*Use caution when parking in an urban environment*," advised the Poe House and Museum website almost ten years later. "*Common sense dictates that you lock your car and keep any valuables out of sight.*" It didn't seem to envisage visitors walking there.

Being urban is our euphemism for being black. When the urban environment was white, we walked there safely.

19. VICARIOUS RACISM

Not until 2013, watching the television series *Power Games*, did I learn that Muslim Indian brothers Arthur and Nizamodeen Hosein, immigrants from Trinidad, kidnapped English housewife Muriel McKay in London in 1969. They'd meant to kidnap newspaper proprietor Rupert Murdoch's wife for ransom. McKay's body was never found.

In spite of having married a Lebanese woman, or perhaps because he had, my school friend Mark's Danish father warned him that Australia opening ourselves to large numbers of Asian immigrants from the 1970s would eventually lead to blood in the streets. Parents can be disruptive influences.

A 2009 survey suggested that sixty-five percent of Australians believed crime had increased through the previous two years, but Australian Institute of Criminology research manager Judy Putt insisted there'd been decreases in theft. (The *Chronicle* newspaper report came with a stock photograph of a young white man with his hands cuffed behind his back.) Such statistics so often touted mean nothing; I'd long stopped bothering to report thefts from my car. New South Wales Bureau of Crime Statistics and Research director Don Weatherburn said of assaults in 2012, "Somewhere around seventy percent don't get reported to the police."

Reverend Gordon Moyes became aware of violent street crime in Harris Park, Sydney as head of Wesley Mission for twenty-seven years to 2005. "I found that over a period of time many elderly Anglo-Saxon women were attacked and robbed and had their purses snatched and phones stolen," he said in 2009. The attacks were primarily carried out by young Australian-born Middle Eastern men brought up in the area. "This has been their turf for as long as they've been alive and now they've got different people moving in – there's a bit of assertion on street areas."

As a New South Wales parliamentarian, he'd raised the issue in parliament in 2007, although I saw no reports of his comments at the time. We don't cater to white people's fears. We call them phobias.

"What has happened over the last few years is that a number of Indian students," Moyes continued in 2009, "attracted by fairly cheap accommodation, have come into the area. The target – always the soft targets – moved from elderly people walking on the street to Indian students with laptops." Since we'd become afraid to walk the streets at night, the people most likely to be outside weren't just those secure within their gangs. They were Indian students headed home from jobs their visas prohibited them from having. "I think elderly Anglos became more cautious in venturing out, and the target shifted to another group."

Indians didn't respond when an Indian raped a fourteen-year-old girl in Burnett Lane, Brisbane the penultimate Sunday in May 2009. The crimes engaging immigrants aren't those their races commit, but those in which they're victims.

Attacks upon Indian students in Australia at the time included assailants calling them "curry eaters." One South Asian wasn't assaulted when thugs discovered he was Pakistani, not Indian. (We didn't imagine that being due to Muslims not assaulting fellow Muslims.)

Indians in India expressed racial solidarity with Indians in Australia inconceivable to us. They directed their anger at white Australians they presumed were responsible, with only Western news reports to go on. Indians in Australia knew more than Indians in India knew. They had their experiences and no reticence in identifying the race of people attacking them. Their protests early in June 2009 blamed Lebanese.

We had no bar of their racism. "The victims of crime that do occur in this area are not exclusively Indian," insisted police superintendent Robert Redfern, as if that should make Indians feel better. "The perpetrators of those crimes are not exclusively Middle Eastern."

Rather than complaining about crime, we were back in our usual Western frenzy about racism. "Racial vilification is a thing of the past," declared television personality Eddie Maguire after the murder of Canadian tourist Cain Aguiar, "to indulge is to become a pariah. So, ladies and gentlemen of Melbourne, are we fair dinkum about wanting to change the violence on our streets?" A further blight on racist white Australia, it didn't matter to Maguire that the men who'd murdered Aguiar were Pacific Islanders.

Being blind to race but not racism, we take responsibility for other people's racism. Closed circuit television of an assault on one Asian student showed several races among the assailants, including another Asian. Many Indian victims described their attackers as being African, Maori, or Islander. Noticing that the crimes and racism for which we're so ashamed aren't committed by white people would be racist.

Our vicarious culpability for other people's crimes isn't a national culpability we carry. It's racial. Neither we nor anyone else impose it upon our citizenry of other races.

Less concerned with education than income, education ministers meeting in Hobart set up a task force to protect the interests of foreign students. (Australian victims hardly rated a mention.) The best way to make Melbourne safer for them would've been to restrict immigration, but we don't countenance that.

Race Discrimination Commissioner Tom Calma, an Aboriginal elder, wasn't concerned about crime or Indians standing loyally with their own. What concerned the ironically named Calma were white Australians again questioning high levels of Asian immigration. "We need to recognise that racism does exist in Australia," he said in 2009. "It doesn't mean the whole society is racist, but it does exist with individual's actions and small group actions. It's important that we all accept that, understand and start to develop the frameworks to address it into the future and not be reactive but be proactive. That is really what I think we are lacking at this stage." I wondered what more we could do.

In spite of most of the assailants being immigrants, historian Robin Jeffrey went so far as to see the attacks as a reminder of the White Australia Policy restricting immigration into Australia to Europeans, effectively abandoned in the 1960s and abolished altogether in 1973. "There is a foundation for Indians' suspicion of Australia on these issues," he said in 2009. (There was no great immigration into India.)

While we fretted about racism, the streets became more dangerous. An international university student walking home from Springvale railway station, Melbourne, shortly after eleven o'clock at night the third Thursday of June 2009, was grabbed from behind. "Stop shouting," Harjot Hundal Singh told her. "Otherwise, I will kill you with a knife." He dragged her into the back of a work van, tied her arms together with rope, hit her several times on the head and neck, squeezed her throat so hard she thought she would die, and raped her.

Psychologist Patrick Newton thought Singh, who'd come to Australia on a spousal visa, attacked her because of his pent up anger towards his mother and wife. At the end of his gaol sentence, he would be deported back to India (for which Indians would presumably accuse us of racism).

Another month later, newspapers reported the sexual assault of a teenage girl asleep on an interstate train by Sukhjinder Singh and Amarjit Singh. The headline called them just "*Two*" without saying two what. Having mentioned their names, the article could hardly call them anything but Indian students.

Nobody conceived racial blame upon Indians as we did upon white people. Indian student Amrick Thind angrily tried to overtake a car in East Bentleigh whose driver had offended him, two days after Christmas 2009. Thind crashed into a four-wheel drive vehicle that then crashed into a car being driven by a woman eight months pregnant, killing her unborn baby.

Indians weren't even concerned when the victims of Indian crime were fellow Indians. They didn't speak up for fruit picker Ranjodh Singh, murdered in Griffith in December 2009 by an Indian couple. Nor did they protest for Chamanjot Singh, killed in her Sydney home four days after Christmas 2009 by her Indian husband. The man charged with the death of three-year-old Gurshan Singh Channa in March 2010, who shared a house with the dead boy and his parents, was also Indian.

What mattered were crimes with Indian victims committed by other races, such as the stabbing murder of Nitin Garg in a Melbourne park the first Saturday of 2010. "This heinous crime on humanity," responded India's external affairs minister Somanahalli Krishna, "this is an uncivilised brutal attack on innocent Indians."

Murder is one thing. Money is something else. Doubtlessly (and needlessly) fearing the economic effect of fewer Indians coming to Australia to study and work, Acting Prime Minister Julia Gillard said there was violence all over the world.

"*Far from admitting to racist horror*," responded the *Times Now* television channel website in India, "*Australia has now come up with an outrageous explanation.*"

There was no evidence Garg's murder was racially motivated,

but when we punish ourselves, other races do too. "This story has redefined the image of Australia for the average TV watcher in India," said Nalin Mehta, a television historian.

An Indian newspaper published a cartoon portraying a Victorian police officer in a Ku Klux Klan uniform. The editor said later the cartoon "helped people focus on the issue" and wasn't intended to label all Australians as racist. He seemed to consider only white Australians to be Australians.

In such an atmosphere, Jaspreet Singh claimed to have been doused with petrol and set alight by a gang in Melbourne in January 2010. He was later charged with making a false police report and criminal damage to gain financial advantage.

The night before Australia Day 2010 in Swanston Street, ten men made racist insults against two Indians, pushed them to the ground, cut one of them with a weapon, and left the other with abrasions. The two assailants not yet arrested meant the first news report, down towards the end of it, mentioned the attackers were Asian.

Six hours later, a revised news report mentioned police charging five men from five different suburbs of Melbourne for the assault. Reference to them being Asian had disappeared.

In February 2010, Malaysian foreign minister Datuk Seri Anifah Aman wanted to know that the murder of Australian citizen Mohd Shah Saemin, living in Sydney, wasn't racially motivated. Saemin was in a car that collided with a black sedan in Cromwell Street, Leichhardt, from which two men leapt, struck him with a hammer, and stabbed him. News reports had already mentioned that one of the two men had curly hair but (as if to comfort Malaysians) added that the murderers' skin was olive.

A day later, New South Wales and Singapore police charged Indonesian Hazairin Iskandar and his son Andrew with murder. Their wife and mother Nita Eriza Iskandar had worked with the victim at the small Malaysian consulate, becoming sexually involved with him. The murder was a family affair: an honour killing.

Being a minor, newspapers couldn't publish the name of the boy Victorian police ultimately charged with Nitin Garg's murder, with any inferences about race it might have conveyed. Preventing the prejudice of Indians against Lebanese necessitated the *Australian* newspaper mentioning this one's race in June 2010. "*The 15-year-old boy, who cannot be identified because of his age, but who is Anglo*

Saxon in appearance with red hair, sat glancing at his tearful mother and father sitting in the front row in a Children's Court."

I couldn't help but think that if the boy had been of any race but European, then his race would've remained irrelevant. Nobody cares about prejudice against white people.

Few things assure us more of our rejection of racism than white criminals. They convince us there would still be crime if our countries had remained racially homogeneous. We then end the thought process, without contemplating the impact interracial immigration has on white people or posing the question whether there might be less crime without particular races.

Really, we wouldn't consider a racial component even if no white person committed a wrongdoing. No other race is guiltier of crime than we are, although we don't disregard white slave masters because other races owned slaves or the Holocaust because other races attempted genocide, even succeeded.

Meanwhile, a man wearing blue jeans, brown suede coat, and thongs grabbed a sixteen-year-old schoolgirl from behind in Gandangara Park, Casula the last Friday in June, 2010. He put his hand down her top, but she resisted him. He thus pushed her to the ground.

A few weeks later, on the third Tuesday in July, the same man grabbed a seventeen-year-old schoolgirl walking in Ledger Street, Casula from behind, this time by the neck, and sexually assaulted her. Making identifying him more difficult, he'd changed his clothes between the attacks. The second time, he wore a black hooded jacket, black Nike hat, and dark tracksuit pants.

Both attacks were in daytime. Both girls described their attacker as being Indian or sub-continental.

Criminals at the time weren't all Indian. That same day as the second assault, two Aboriginal or Torres Strait Islander men knocked on the door of a home in Doonside. They struck the man answering the door with a replica firearm. They threatened his mother, forced him into his bedroom, and struck him with a golf club.

Nor were Indians responsible for all abduction attempts in Casula. Two months later, in September 2010, an East Asian grabbed a thirteen-year-old boy walking along Leacocks Lane to the bus stop by his tee shirt and dragged him away. The boy broke free and fled.

While other races are furious to think we're prejudiced against them, we have no problems with their prejudices against us. *"Ugly Australians aren't just confined to the cricket field,"* declared one Indian newspaper, reported Australian journalist Peter Lalor in October 2010.

"In truth," commented Lalor, as if it were the truth, *"Indians have every right to be hostile and suspicious toward us, when they regularly read of their countrymen being bashed in the xenophobic lowlands of Melbourne."* No white person rushed to our defence as other races rush to theirs. *"Perhaps we had better get used to the ugly Aussie tag. It could be worse."*

So Tosha Thakkar was forever described as an Indian accountancy student assaulted, raped, strangled with a black coaxial cable, and stuffed into a suitcase by her neighbour in Sydney suburban Croydon in March 2011. News reports only ever called her murderer Daniel Stani Reginald, who took a taxi to Meadowbank and dumped the suitcase in a canal, a Sydney storeman. Court records from his father murdering his mother a decade earlier revealed he was Sri Lankan.

At one o'clock in the morning the first Thursday in January 2012, Khalil Balluch was driving home to Auburn with his brother and sister-in-law. Along Hassall Street, Harris Park, his car ran out of petrol, whereby up to fifteen men appeared and set upon the three, stabbing Balluch in the stomach. They demanded his car keys only to be told the car had no petrol, so they set upon him again before running away with his wallet and telephone.

"It appears to be an opportunistic attack and unlucky for" the victim "being in the wrong place at the wrong time," said police inspector George Radmore. The *Australian Broadcasting Corporation News* at seven o'clock that evening didn't mention the assailants' races, nor did the first report from the *Sydney Morning Herald* newspaper. The *Daily Telegraph* newspaper did. After all, the police were looking for them. They were Pacific Islanders. Hassall Street, Harris Park so late at night had become their place.

20. VICTIMS OF COLOUR

As part of the Multicultural Perspectives Public Speaking Competition at our local primary school in 2011, my second son told me a contestant spoke of some Muslim girls being beaten up. The audience didn't know the girls, but that wasn't the point. Its sympathy wasn't supposed to be directed to those girls individually or girls collectively, but Muslims. Whether the story was true didn't matter.

White girls being beaten up wouldn't have been within the spirit of the competition. Crimes by others against white people involve no social issues we want to explore. Indeed, quite the opposite: the last thing we want to do is promote white people's racism.

On the third Thursday in July 2010, a robbery at the Uriage-les-Bains casino led to a car chase in which the robbers shot at French police at least three times. Police defending themselves killed a robber, whose memorial service the next day provoked riots. Shortly before midnight on Friday, around thirty youths armed with baseball bats and iron bars seized a tram in the working-class La Villeneuve neighbourhood of Grenoble, ordering passengers to leave. When police intervened, the youths began torching between fifty and sixty cars, looting construction equipment and two shops, and attacking police, who responded with tear gas. At about two thirty Saturday morning, a rioter shot at police. Police returned fire four times.

The French government vowed to crackdown on "delinquents," a lovely term I recalled referring to small boys stealing apples from apple trees. There was no mention of race or religion, although the dead robber, who already had three convictions for armed robbery, was Karim Boudouda.

For the race, religion, or immigration status of other races involved in crime or other wrongdoing to be relevant, they need to be not the criminal but the victim. Britain's refusal to compile statistics of the race or religion of criminals doesn't deter the Home Office from publishing statistics of anti-Semitic hate crimes and, since 2015, hate crimes against Muslims.

Bayok Makuer having been a Sudanese refugee when he arrived in Australia with his wife and child was central to the story of twenty African construction workers not receiving superannuation entitlements, penalty rates, holidays, sick pay, or safety inductions. (We don't just grant refuge. We grant holidays.) They'd been paid in cash, which let them avoid paying income taxes and continue receiving all government assistance, but they wanted more. Seven years later, with four children, Makuer was complaining about the pay he'd not received.

The director of D & G Group which employed them, Daniel Deng Lual, was also Sudanese. The named director of Fyna Formwork, which appointed D & G, was Stephen Soong.

I was surprised to see an Australian news headline candidly report a Burmese refugee guilty of assault in 2012, until I read the article. Harroon Rashid had assaulted staff and damaged property to the tune of sixteen thousand dollars at a Northern Territory immigration detention centre. A magistrate sentenced him to ten months in gaol, but then suspended the sentence because he felt that uncertainty and prolonged detention (because security officers had been unable to clear Rashid of being a threat) contributed to his actions.

The substance of the story wasn't a refugee assaulting people. It was a refugee being a victim of detention.

'Rapist destroyed migrant's dream,' decried the *Advertiser* newspaper after Lindsay Goldsmith raped a Botswanan immigrant in her Adelaide home in 2007. Without hint of the rapist's race, the only image of him was an artist's ambiguous sketch. There was only his name, age, and that he'd spent thirteen of his thirty-three years in gaol.

Reports of Joan Ryther's murder at Logan in Queensland in 2013 made much of the victim being Filipina. I'd assumed the young murderer was white Australian, as I assumed his supporters gathering outside the court were (although it's hard to imagine white people supporting each other), until I read a single reference to an appeal for calm among those supporters by an Aboriginal elder.

I'd met human rights lawyer Graeme Innes with his daughter one Sunday morning several of us planted trees at St Ives Showground. Since then, he'd become the Australian Human

Rights Commission's Disability Discrimination Commissioner, Human Rights Commissioner, and Race Discrimination Commissioner. Innes wasn't merely colour-blind, but blind. The allegations of racially motivated attacks against Indians led him in 2010 to complain that there was "no national data on the prevalence of migrants as victims of crime."

He proposed racial profiling not of criminals but victims. "Racial profiling perpetrators, however," he said, "is little more than a guess, which often reinforces incorrect stereotypes."

The distinction was curious, but Innes' motivation wasn't preventing crime. If it wasn't assuring Indians they could come safely to Australia, it was averting white people's racism.

Addressing the committee of the United Nations International Convention on the Elimination of All Forms of Racial Discrimination (which would be more accurately titled one for the Elimination of All Forms of *White* Racial Discrimination) in Geneva in August that year, Innes called for changes to the Australian Constitution – the most important document in the country – to give greater effect to laws against racism. He wanted federal law to criminalise racial hatred.

In August 2009, the *Sydney Morning Herald* newspaper reported a series of disappearances and murders involving Asian victims since November 2008. The article didn't mention the perpetrators' races, although it was about the growing workload of the Asian Crime Squad. (The squad wasn't named for the races of the victims.)

In 2010, the newspaper blazed away with a touching and beautiful photograph of Yanna Fang and her late husband Jiang Ming Hai, with what looked like a very Sydney coastal backdrop. She'd told the New South Wales Supreme Court of her "lifetime sentence of endless sorrow and indescribable pain" after he was brutally murdered in suburban North Ryde. "Seeing a bathtub is a brutal reminder of how his already dead and lifeless body was submerged," were the widow's words. "I had the bathtub removed, and when in close proximity of a hammer I experience panic attacks for which no amount of medication or counselling can diminish."

She said her husband had been her soulmate. "He proved to me that true happiness existed by being himself – happy, outgoing, warm hearted and most of all kind and gentle." At the time of his murder, she and their children had been in China. In their last telephone conversation, they'd spoken of "renewing our marriage vows with our children and family."

She read out a poem that began: "The most I miss him is late at night, when I want him there to hold me tight." Her heart ached for their children especially when she heard other youngsters call out for their father. "One night, my three-year-old daughter discovered our wedding photos. I asked her if she remembered her Dad and her reply ripped out my heart – that if she mentioned him, I will cry." She didn't agree that time healed all wounds. "My pain, like my love for my husband, will never be gone but will be for all eternity."

Never had I read so much of the pain in the spouse of a white murder victim. The murderer was incidental. He was handyman Jian Dong.

To promote tolerance of other races and deal with issues of racism, we're not shy to mention the races of white criminals and victims of colour. Nothing's better than when they come together: white mischief.

Jacqueline Woodhouse wasn't the first person to board a London underground train intoxicated, when she did so one evening in January 2012. Nor was she the first to berate her fellow passengers with profanities, except that hers included racial insults. "You Africans take our council flats," she told Judy Russell, for example.

Her abuse lasted seven minutes, which Galbant Juttla filmed on his mobile telephone. He told Woodhouse to keep her mouth shut, and that she'd drunk too much alcohol.

"It's not your country anyway, so what's your problem?" she replied. "It's been overtaken by people like you."

"I found it very distressing," Juttla said later, although not so distressing as to deter him from loading the recording of Woodhouse onto the YouTube website. The whole world could thus see and hear her. "I uploaded it to YouTube because I thought that was the fast-track process to catching this person," he explained. "I also needed to show the public that kind of person is out there, and not to put up with this kind of behaviour."

"Anyone viewing it," said District Judge Michael Snow of the recording, "would feel a deep sense of shame that our citizens could be subject to such behaviour who may, as a consequence, believe that it secretly represents the views of other white people."

That was to say, he worried about racism other white people hid.

At a time when we search for reasons to avoid incarcerating most criminals, we're looking for reasons to incarcerate racists. We offer them none of the leniency we offer hoods and rapists. Woodhouse pleaded guilty to racially aggravated intentional harassment, for which Snow sentenced her to twenty-one weeks in gaol.

'Kenya court finds white aristocrat guilty of manslaughter,' declared the *Sydney Morning Herald* in 2009. Blacks had complained of racism when black prosecutors dropped charges of murder after an earlier killing in which Thomas Cholmondeley said he acted in self-defence. With no more than the testimony of one person, prosecutors laid charges of murder against him for the death of Robert Njoya, a suspected poacher, before lay assessors said the charges should be dropped for lack of evidence.

We're not as tolerant of white people's crimes as we tolerate those of other races. Extensive media coverage of the murder of Stephen Lawrence at a bus stop in Eltham, London in 1993 and of the trial of the accused murderer never failed to mention Lawrence was black and the group that set upon him was white. "What?" asked one. "What, nigger?" The worst of all criminals are racist white criminals.

Among the inquiries and inquisitions, one by Senior Judge William Macpherson published in 1999 decided the London Metropolitan Police and British policing in general was "institutionally racist." Macpherson's recommendations changed the way police handled murders of black people.

America late in 2013 suffered a spate of attacks by people knocking strangers in the street unconscious, severely injuring many and reportedly killing one. Assailants seemed to be black and victims white, although few news reports alluded to race beyond the photographs. None published any statistics. No authorities prosecuted assailants for hate crimes, until New York authorities charged one in November for targeting a Jew.

In December, the Department of Justice filed a criminal complaint against a white man, Conrad Alvin Barrett, for allegedly targeting a black man in Texas. "The plan is to see if I were to hit a black person, would this be nationally televised?" Barrett had asked in a video recording. It was.

White criminals' racism we make central to their identity. We've no worries about people making negative generalisations about racist white people. We want it.

We thus read every detail of the abuse by a group of people against David Chia outside his home in Pymble, early the third Saturday of January 2006. "I'm going to kill you," yelled Shaun Wickenden, "you gook."

Wickenden was convicted of assault and fined a thousand dollars. Furthermore, Judge Ray McLoughlin in the New South Wales District Court awarded Chia more than a hundred and thirty thousand dollars, including seventy-five thousand dollars in general damages and forty thousand dollars in aggravated and exemplary damages.

Nor was there any hesitation in reporting the words of Clinton Rintoull about Melbourne in 2007. "These blacks are turning this town into the Bronx," he shouted. "I'm going to take my town back. I'm looking to kill the blacks." He killed a Sudanese man.

Traumatic experiences excusing crime by other races don't excuse crime by racist white people. Three days before the killing, Rintoull had entered a derelict house offering a sandwich to help an African boy. Twenty Sudanese, most likely from a Sudanese gang operating from the Noble Park railway station, some carrying knives, chased him away.

Poor white people often seem sad and lonely figures, without gangs or their race to stand with them, estranged from everyone. 'Racist who plotted tennis ball bombings convicted,' headed a 2009 *Sydney Morning Herald* article, never shy to define white people by racism. I don't know whether the description "*white supremacist*" was one that English electrician Neil Lewington gave himself or someone else gave him. He'd planned to throw bombs in tennis balls into the homes of Asian families in England.

We're not so fussed about bigotry from people of other races. Ivan Wong noticed a Korean among a group of three Koreans staring at him in the World Square shopping centre, Sydney the third Thursday morning in March 2008. He later returned with a friend, Michael Lee, carrying a knife and a hammer. After waiting for the Koreans to leave a fast-food restaurant, they chased Joon Yup Lee into a lane. "Are you Korean?" Michael Lee twice asked him, striking him with the hammer. Michael Lee held him while Wong stabbed him four times, including a fatal blow to his heart.

News reports made no mention of the killers' race, but their surnames suggested or showed them to be Chinese. Sentencing Michael Lee in the New South Wales Supreme Court, Judge Derek Price believed he'd shown remorse and co-operated with police. The judge felt he had good prospects of rehabilitation.

We can't seem to imagine rehabilitating white racists. Upon them, we impose exemplary damages.

In 2008, shortly before Christmas, fifteen-year-old Tyler Cassidy stole two knives from a Kmart department store in Melbourne. Soon afterwards, armed with those knives, he threatened one of two policemen in All Nations Park in suburban Northcote. Those policemen shot and killed him.

Had he not been white, Cassidy's race would've been irrelevant to the crime he committed, although not to being killed by police. Instead, emblazoned across the news was Cassidy's membership of a white nationalist group Southern Cross Soldiers and its words on the My Space website. *"This is about how we walk down the main street in any town or city in Australia and see more foreign flags than we do Aussie, hear more foreign languages than we do English, in all honesty it's about the fact that we as true Australians are becoming the minority in OUR own country!"*

I couldn't help but contrast our responses to other criminals with our derision for racist white criminals. We don't indulge them their crimes for their poverty or other problems; the defences we offer other races we don't offer our own. We expect white people to embrace multiculturalism, while helping other races along. If Cassidy felt out of place in multiracial Australia, as those writings suggested, we give him no sympathies. Policemen defending their lives can no more care what motivates a boy preparing to kill them than I would, but the troubled young Cassidy might have gone out that day wanting police to kill him cold.

21. LIES

If the overwhelming evidence of racial diversity is negative, that only makes seizing upon faint flickers of anything positive more important. The first Wednesday in August 2008, a fourteen-year-old boy walking home from school in St Marys was grabbed from behind. A man punched him in the stomach and pulled him towards a white Mercedes van, before the boy broke free and ran away. With police still looking for the man, a news report described him as being "*of Pacific Islander appearance*," but the assailant wasn't the focus of the report. It was the plucky youngster fending him off. The news was good.

If nothing's positive, we make it up. The truth is immaterial.

In the 1990s, New South Wales deputy police commissioner Jeff Jarratt led a committee that created a special crime index showing that prosperous white Roseville suffered more crime than Vietnamese Cabramatta. It did so by excluding drug crime and murder. Police officer Tim Priest revealed police were told to ignore the crime they saw each day in Cabramatta. There were no such instructions in Roseville.

Little crime in Cabramatta was reported until the 2012 television documentary *Once Upon a Time in Cabramatta*, but that was another story of immigrant success. "*In the mid-'90s,*" said the television guide, "*the Vietnamese enclave of Cabramatta was in trouble: gangs controlled the streets, heroin turned it into the smack capital of Australia, and it was the scene of the only political assassination in Australian history.*" (There'd been no such doomsaying then. There'd been only denial.) "*But 15 years later, Cabramatta is a shining multicultural triumph. This is the inside story of how a newly arrived migrant community was torn apart by crime but fought back to rediscover itself and forge a successful future.*"

Race isn't relevant to crime at the time. It becomes relevant to stories later of crime being overcome.

The Vietnamese enjoyed the credit for such supposed success although a day earlier, I'd read sociologist Andrew Jakubowicz (who apparently appeared in the programme) blame the problems suffered by newer immigrant groups on a lack of government support. The problems are our fault. Overcoming the problems are the immigrants' achievements. They're themes for Harmony Day.

Also in 2012, the *Sydney Morning Herald* had no trouble categorising Telopea Street, Punchbowl as having been "*home to Sydney's worst violence, drug dealing and criminality*," but that was ten years earlier. The street became newsworthy not for the crime never reported at the time, but for the end of crime. When we acknowledge the bedlam, it's not the bedlam that's there but the bedlam that used to be.

Telopea Street had been a criminal street without criminal races, although all the criminals and all but one of the victims mentioned were Arabs. That victim was Asian. If there'd been fault it wasn't by race but by age. "Before, yeah," said Mohammad Dib, "there was drug dealing and stuff, but we were young guys misled by older guys." He'd spent eight years in gaol for altering stolen cars to mask their past ownership and trying to hide his fifteen-year-old brother's role in murdering schoolboy Edward Lee in a brawl on the street.

By 2012, Telopea Street was supposedly all very lovely. If crime had moved, it hadn't moved far.

A day after the article, Ali Eid (a father of four) and Mohammed Hanouf were working on Eid's unfinished two-storey mansion in Lumeah Avenue, Punchbowl. Just after four o'clock that afternoon, two masked gunmen clothed in black shot the two men from behind, killing Eid, before fleeing to the street. Heavily armed police officers, dogs, and helicopters searched the area without finding them, with residents and workers ordered to stay inside and lock their doors. A few weeks later, Eid's relative Bachir Ajra would be shot dead outside his family home, also in Punchbowl.

Trying to curtail the conflicts and frictions of racial diversity, we withhold information. In 2015, Sudanese immigrants gang raped a female "No Borders" activist working to help them in an immigrant camp in Ponte San Ludovico in Ventimiglia, Italy. She remained silent for more than a month because "the others asked me to keep quiet," fearing it would set back their struggle for a borderless world. When she did report the rape, her fellow activists accused her of doing so out of spite because her group left the camp following an unrelated controversy.

What we can't conceal, we distort. We lie.

Afghan asylum seeker Ahadullah Khughiani arrived in Britain in 2008. Enjoying government payments, he'd been in the country only a few months when he was among five men who abducted a woman walking near her home in Bristol. They raped her, laughing and joking together as they did. The deoxyribonucleic acid (D.N.A.) taken from him on arrival meant he was caught and convicted. "This was an extremely rare incident," claimed detective inspector Will White of Avon and Somerset police. "We don't want the public to be unduly fearful because of this one incident."

"*Due to my profession*," commented Mad Max on the *Sun* newspaper website, "*I can tell you with authority that this most certainly is not a rare incident as the police spokesman claimed.*"

Unverifiable as they often are, anonymous website postings aren't ideal sources of information. They're often all we have.

Sometimes, we have more. Sitting next to a Coffs Harbour policeman at a wedding, our friend Jenna learnt of that city's high crime rate due largely to refugees and the unemployed.

A lack of statistics about race and religion in crime doesn't deter politicians and police spokesmen and women in Britain from lying. Having such statistics isn't a reason for police commissioners in Australia to be truthful, when they're the wrong sorts of statistics.

"Sudanese refugees are actually under-represented in the crime statistics," claimed Victorian police commissioner Christine Nixon in 2007, amidst the cries of protest after Australian immigration minister Kevin Andrews spoke of violence by Sudanese. In fact, her private data showed Sudanese to be four times more likely than everyone else to be charged with crimes.

Lying has become a legitimate public policy tool. It never does contestants any harm in multicultural speaking competitions.

If good beauty pageants alleviate the tedium of white people's lives, they're nothing compared to what they do for Africans. South Australia convened its first Miss Africa beauty pageant in October 2010, when a hundred and fifty Africans spilled out of a nightclub into Hindley Street. Four suffered stab wounds during a day of violence.

Later, up to a hundred Africans armed with knives, tyre levers, clubs, batons, and a bedpost fought a pitched battle in Bent Street near the Austral Hotel. "Clearly they had prepared themselves with weapons in the event that they did come together," said police chief inspector John Gerlach, "which they did."

The only crime the *Adelaide Advertiser* newspaper mentioned was a spate of carjacking incidents. South Australian police sought a suspect of Aboriginal appearance.

The same day, I read Australian lawyer Jason Pobjoy call upon the West to accept more refugees. *"Australia's international responsibilities extend beyond the provision of financial aid. For some children – and I speak here of the children I encountered in Uganda – financial aid will not suffice… These children need the international community – developed nations such as Australia – to step in and provide surrogate protection."* I'm not sure if he envisaged more beauty pageants.

The last Saturday night in April 2011 saw the Miss South Sudan Australia beauty pageant in Melbourne. Up to a thousand people attended a party at Clayton Town Hall the next afternoon (Anzac Day, for Australians), at which no alcohol was to be served and ten security guards were on hand. Still, the party erupted into a fight. A man with abrasions to his ear took himself to hospital. Another went to help a friend brawling with approximately fifteen Sudanese men aged in their twenties. He was attacked with a machete, hit in the mouth with the blade, stabbed in the hand three times, and suffered welts when struck on the back with a bicycle chain.

The first police to arrive were pelted with glass bottles. Twelve police and three dog squad units took two hours to break up the melee.

"I was really upset that there was a fight," a pageant organiser Phillip told radio station 3AW, "because at the end of the day it is just damaging the reputation of our community."

He needn't have worried. We have Harmony Day.

That night, two groups of South Sudanese drinking alcohol in the Pennell Reserve on Burke Street, Braybrook, near Braybrook College and Braybrook Primary School, broke into a fight on the oval with weapons. Police arrived in response at about twenty minutes to two o'clock early Monday morning, when as many as a hundred South Sudanese turned on police, pelting them with glass stubby bottles, striking an officer on the back of the head and cutting another on the nose. The crowd threw rocks and bottles at a police divisional van (used for transporting criminals) and kicked it.

Police withdrew, calling for help from the Critical Incident

Response Team. The Sudanese again fought each other. One was taken to the Royal Melbourne Hospital with stab wounds to his leg and arm.

Later, with traffic still closed at the corner of Burke Street and Mullenger Road, police superintendent John Hendrickson blamed the violence on alcohol. "Our relationship with the Sudanese community locally has been good," he claimed, "and we have not had many incidents of this nature."

Kymlee Le, who operated a clothing business opposite the reserve, refuted him. She said the Sudanese held wild parties at a hall there every weekend. "They fight a lot of the time," she said. "I can see a lot of different…, not Australian." If she was white, she would have been racist. "I'm scared. After they drink they wreck the bottle and hit each other. It makes a lot of problems. Every Monday we come here and we clean all the area because you can see so many broken bottles." Her shop windows had been damaged five times in the past four years.

The next night was the turn of Daisey's Hotel on Mount Dandenong Road, Ringwood. Around ten thirty, about thirty young Africans, all apparently intoxicated, brawled in the car park. When police arrived, the Africans ran to Ringwood Lake Park and continued fighting, leaving among the injured in the car park a man who refused treatment from paramedics. He returned to the fighting and was bashed unconscious. An hour after refusing their help, the paramedics found him conscious, with bruising and swelling to his face and an injury to his leg.

A Victoria Police spokeswoman said those involved in that third fight in as many nights "appeared to have been alcohol affected and have been unco-operative with police." It was another delightful understatement, characterising our culturally sensitive treatment of crime.

"Every police commissioner and interior minister will deny it," said Bernhard Witthaut, Germany's chief police commissioner by 2011, "but of course we know where we can go with the police car." Those weren't the areas with large numbers of immigrants. Police "can no longer feel safe there in twos, and have to fear becoming the victim of a crime themselves… Even worse: in these areas, crimes no longer result in charges. They are left to themselves. Only in the worst cases do we in the police learn anything about it. The power of the state is completely out of the picture."

When American presidential candidate Donald Trump said in 2015 that police could no longer enter parts of Britain because of Muslims, Britain's Prime Minister David Cameron called Trump's statements "divisive, unhelpful, and quite simply wrong."

The Metropolitan Police insisted Trump "could not be more wrong."

London mayor Boris Johnson said Trump's claims were "utter nonsense."

Yet the previous year, Her Majesty's chief inspector of constabulary Tom Winsor told the *Times* newspaper there were "cities in the Midlands where the police never go," because there were "communities from other cultures who would prefer to police themselves." British police "don't know what injustices are being perpetrated."

Ordinary police officers confirmed the truth of Trump's words. Writing in the Police Community forum, one London officer said Trump was *"pointing out something plainly obvious, something which...we aren't as a nation willing to own up to..."*

An officer with Lancashire police said police had to "contact local community leaders to get their permission," before they were allowed to patrol Muslim areas of Preston.

A Yorkshire policeman wrote that police fears of terrorist attacks led to him being ordered not to wear his police uniform in his patrol car, but *"as soon as someone points out the obvious its 'divisive'... Our political leaders are best either ill-informed or simply being disingenuous."*

"Islamification has and is occurring," said a serving officer in west London. "You have to have extra vigilance in certain parts when you are working."

Police and others report areas in Britain, France, Sweden, and elsewhere police can no longer safely work. The most senior police and politicians deny such areas exist.

We trumpet multiculturalism as the purveyor of greatness, but the compliments we give ourselves only make our lies more pervasive. After the 2012 presentation day at my eldest son's high school, the head of the parents and citizens association told me people assumed he was racist because he spoke with a South African accent. They, including a politician who'd spoken in parliament against racism, freely opened up with all manner of racial complaints.

We rebuke people who don't lie as we lie, trying desperately to achieve our global ideal. We hide in our skin hoping nobody knows our secret-most thoughts; shouting each other down means we can't hear our whispers. We pretend so much, but demonise anyone who suggests we're pretending.

Our postmodern West might all be a lie, our lives complete lies. It's so hard to know. We don't know what the secrets are.

Little wonder, our children disbelieve us. The product of a government education, with years of Harmony Days and Multicultural Perspectives Public Speaking Competitions behind her, my eldest daughter honoured all our multiracial edicts and counted Asians and a Muslim girl among her friends. I thus had many reasons to be surprised by a joke she told me was passed around a school friend's party their last day of fifth class. "There were three people on a 'plane," the joke began, "not including the pilot: an American, a Chinese, and an Australian. The 'plane was getting too heavy, so the pilot said 'everybody drop something that your country has a lot of.'

"The American said 'I'll drop a hamburger, because my country has too many of those.'

"The Chinese man said 'I'll drop this fragrance, because my country has too many of these.'

"The Australian man said 'I'll drop this Chinese man, because my country has *way* too many of them.'" That was affection aside the jokes she later told me the boys at her high school made about Aborigines.

Knowing what white people think about race, our decline, and the changes under way across the West is difficult. With few people with whom to confide, I'm not sure of the extent to which any of us speak freely. Much as East Europeans did in the days of communism, rather than suffering the aggravation of people outside censoring for us, we learn to say what we must.

When all other censorship is in place, the last is self-censorship inside people's heads. We don't consider what we've learnt we're forbidden to say. People who believe what we ought to believe are most likely to say what we ought to say. People who question and speak aloud of their questions will almost certainly utter them wrongly. We've lost our chance for undisciplined thoughts. If we're not careful, we might think.

Without freedom of speech, we have no freedom of thought,

nor freedom to feel. Our right is to believe what others want us to believe. The most complete censorship is within people's souls.

22. THE LONELIEST PEOPLE
ON EARTH

At the 2012 Multicultural Day for my elder daughters' high school, the *Sydney Morning Herald* newspaper photographer wanted a picture of children in the Chinese room, but only after asking my middle daughter's friend Isabella to move away because she wasn't Asian. Isabella was upset, but the purpose of Multicultural Day wasn't to make white people feel included. Not everyone belonged, after all.

While we encourage children of other races to be proud of their race, we belittle our race to our children. In a multicultural speaking competition at primary school, my pretty youngest daughter spoke of being a mix of English, Scottish, Welsh, and Irish. A teacher told her she needed "ethnic spice."

Immigrants are at the forefront of celebrating multiculturalism and our other national celebrations too. My youngest daughter wanted to read the poem at her primary school's commemoration of the centenary of the Anzac landing at Gallipoli, but the teacher was unwilling to deny the Asian girl Elissa her wish to do so, in spite of Elissa already playing the piano at the event. The teacher instructed the girls to play the scissors, paper, rock game, in which Elissa saw that my daughter's and her choices would have meant she lost, so she hurriedly changed her choice. My daughter knew better than to tell the teacher that an Asian girl had cheated.

We persevere, whatever circumstances befall us. We keep moving along, trying to get through the days and weeks as well we can.

In the 2015 multicultural speaking competition, my youngest daughter spoke of being British: Irish, English, Scottish, and Welsh. Her teacher awarded her twenty-eight marks out of thirty, with his sole criticism being that she should have been more multicultural. (No child of another race describing his or her identity was criticised for being racially pure.) Hearing my wife tell her about it, the penultimate Sunday in May, my mother-in-law apologised for not being multiracial.

THE FAILURE OF MULTICULTURALISM

A year later, my daughter spoke of several other races as well as her own, but was still told her speech wasn't sufficiently multicultural. Perhaps she shouldn't have mentioned the British at all.

"When our kids see themselves reflected in school," Wiradjuri woman Leila Smith told National Indigenous Television, Australia in 2025," they show up stronger and they dream bigger." She was talking about Indigenous Australians participating in the Redefining Indigenous Success in Education programme, but it was true of Western children too.

There's every good reason to make the best of life by seeing the positives in things we can't change. We see only the benefits of racial diversity because we feel we have no choice but to accept it, but our inviolate presumption wasn't one our forebears made, the rest of the world makes, or interracial immigrants make about the countries they leave behind. Ours are the democracies of the world, in which we consent to being powerless. If we imagine being empowered, if only in the sanctuary of our minds, then we can question whether the West needs multiculturalism.

Sometime around 2003, a speaker at a Liberal Party state council meeting mentioned Asian immigrants bringing heroin and other lethal drugs into Australia. Cutting off any line of thought he might have left behind in the audience, a Chinese woman angrily told him he shouldn't dare talk about Asians bringing drugs into Australia after the British brought opium to China. Unusually, her words were an instant of someone else shutting a white person down before fellow white people had the chance to do so. No other speaker dared take up the issue.

European colonialism had long ended; there are no more immigrants in China. They're in Britain. The first speaker had spoken of his life in the present day. The Chinese woman protested passionately about events almost two centuries earlier in a country she might never have seen. The Opium Wars had been from 1839 to '42 and from 1856 to '60. She defended her race, as we don't defend ours. Neither Chinese nor we tolerate our past failings.

I could imagine white people readily believing the Chinese woman was right and tormenting themselves in shame, while we fob off any suggestion the first speaker was right. Her protestation assumed he was. In effect, the Chinese woman was saying that Britain's former colonies shouldn't complain about Chinese immigration harming us because British colonialism harmed China. It's their redress. In fact, the Chinese don't need their experience of opium or other unpleasant, awful, or even fatal consequences of immigration to refuse immigration, although we'd respect such a rationale for others we wouldn't allow ourselves.

Asians and drugs came back to mind in 2008. As we'd been doing for decades, newspaper columnist Elizabeth Farrelly blamed Sydney inner-city Redfern being such a mess not on the Aborigines who lived there but on neglect by white people who didn't. Without concern for the colour in her language, she called it a *"whitewash."*

What made her article so intriguing was the revelation, hidden in her words without race, that ours isn't the only racism. Farrelly described her encounter with a young couple walking through Redfern, the woman struggling with her high-heeled shoes. "Take them off," suggested Farrelly, "go barefoot."

"Not round here," the man replied on the woman's behalf. "Not with the Abos everywhere, all the needles in the streets." He labelled Aborigines (abbreviating language as John Elliott would do) as heroin users. "Be all right when they get rid of the blacks."

My knowledge of people was reason enough to suppose that white people wouldn't be so overt with their racism in front of a stranger. (Save for Elliott's error, we'd learnt to confine it to private conversations with people we knew and South Africans.) *"The couple's ethnicity is irrelevant,"* wrote Farrelly, anticipating my presumption. *"Suffice to note a strong resemblance to the smack-sellers who run my back lane."* Smack was a slang term for heroin. *"Second generation, I'd guess – city workers who have snapped up one of Redfern's smart new apartments."*

They were probably East Asian. Europeans had been in Australia for many more generations than two. Africans, Arabs, South Asians, and Islanders weren't buying smart new apartments. I could have surmised from my knowledge of drug trafficking elsewhere that the couple was Chinese or Vietnamese, but that would've been racist of me.

Farrelly wasn't bothered by Asian drug trafficking as much as by Aboriginal squalor. Her words may well have been directed at that young couple, who'd denigrated Aborigines for taking drugs their race supplied to them. Tactfully, Farrelly warded them away from making more racist remarks against Aborigines, while maintaining her restraint from making racist remarks of her own. She meant to avert racism against their race as much as against Aborigines.

I suspect Farrelly's thoughts never reached so far as to wonder if Asian immigration harmed Aborigines. All she and the young couple had in common was that none of them displayed consideration for the impact of drugs or anything else upon the West. I suspect she'd not have cared about the young couple's racism had it been directed against white people instead of Aborigines.

Nineteen years earlier, one Saturday evening in 1989, I accompanied my friend Colleen Howard and her Jesus Cares ministry colleagues providing bread, cakes, and coffee to the poor of inner Sydney. Government-built homes for Aborigines had fallen to ruin and would in time be demolished. We were probably a few streets away from what would become the smart new apartments Elizabeth Farrelly mentioned.

The stone kerb and gutter at which I sat with some Aboriginal girls overhearing Western music might have been by the footpath where Farrelly would observe that young couple. There were no sights or smells of drugs that I noticed or realised, but there were many other kerbs and gutters in Redfern. I don't recall mention of drugs or drug taking.

The Jesus Cares ministry had no problems with Aborigines. It was there to feed them, after all.

Neither the girls nor I mentioned national issues seizing the minds of political leaders at the time, such as the commemorations the previous year for the Bicentenary of the First Fleet establishing the British colony that became Australia; no great political minds sat with us that night. I never acknowledged any traditional owners, their elders past or present, of the kerb on which we sat; the street would have been bush when the First Fleet arrived. We talked about music.

The Aboriginal girls enjoyed each other and wealthy white people wanting to help them. Those wealthy white people were not with us that night.

Elsewhere that night, Colleen and her group gave food and coffee to prostitutes spaced out near the wall of the old Darlinghurst Gaol, with little to say. White men, women, and children by a cemetery in Newtown were simply poor, but their poverty strained them as it did not strain Aboriginal children. They were alone, apart from each other.

In the basement of an abandoned old building, several young white people squatted. They sat and lay on worn mattresses, hauled there from other people's discarded rubbish. Among them was a woman who might previously have been pretty, lying stretched out on her bed on the floor. By a lighted candle was a spoon, in which she'd cooked her heroin.

She was our citizen of the world, without a country to keep her or a people to care. She was our Western individual, abjectly vulnerable, without a race in which to believe or history to hold, at least that anybody wanted. She had her rights, as did the people who'd brought those drugs to her grasp, but rights don't make people smile.

People in that room might have considered themselves a community, but their community was small, without any person powerful or rich. They had no government to call on for anything but welfare payments. The West that could've cared for them had the world for which to worry, every human being and even animals to help. White people have become the saddest, loneliest people on earth.

Two generations earlier, that young woman unconscious on the mattress had an empire, country, and race, probably a family. She could have worn a nice dress with a hat and talked with unfamiliar people on a bus. She would have smiled at strangers she passed, possibly carrying an umbrella to shield her white skin from the sun. They cared about each other as compatriots did, rather than fretting about everyone else. We now look back with horror they did.

An ambulance came. We saw several ambulances that night. Before morning, the young woman was dead.

BIBLIOGRAPHY, REFERENCES

Articles

Akerman, Pia, 'Mum raped by seven as her kids slept nearby,' *The Australian* newspaper, 15 January 2011.

Allen, Nick, 'California gunman One Goh 'an angry loner who hated women',' *The Telegraph* newspaper, 4 April 2012.

Atfield, Cameron, 'Circus acrobat accused of spreading HIV,' *The Brisbane Times* newspaper, 25 May 2010. Lisa Martin, 'HIV positive Acrobat may have had 'hundreds of partners',' *Australian Associated Press* news service published at *News Limited Network*, 26 May 2010.

Baker, Rebecca and others, 'Dispute over Muslim headwear sends scores of police to Playland; park closed to new visitors,' *The Journal News*, 31 August 2011.

Bevan, Edith, 'Eddie was killed because he did not have a cigarette,' *The Daily Telegraph* newspaper, 22 April 2008. Margaret Scheikowski, 'Boy, 15, jailed 16 years for murder of innocent bystander,' *Australian Associated Press* news service published at *News Limited Network*, 21 May 2010.

Bibby, Paul, "A terrible way to die': storeman jailed for murdering Indian neighbour,' *The Sydney Morning Herald* newspaper, 17 May 2013.

Birbalsingh, Katherine, 'These riots were about race. Why ignore the fact?' *Daily Telegraph* newspaper, 7 August 2011, with comments by Brian Schoneker, Albert1818, and Leo S on 10 August 2011. Alexandra Topping, 'Looting 'fuelled by social exclusion',' *The Guardian* newspaper, 9 August 2011. Nino Bucci, 'Weep for all our futures: toxic mix feeds riots,' *The Sydney Morning Herald* newspaper, 10 August 2011. Mary Riddell, 'Riots: the underclass lashes out,' *The Telegraph* newspaper, 8 August 2011. Uncredited, 'Social media in spotlight as Blackberry, Twitter come under fire during London riots,' *News Limited Network*, 9 August 2011. Adrian Croft, 'Schools, jobs seen key to prevent repeat of English riots,' *Reuters* news service, 28 March 2012.

Bloxham, Andy, 'Children snatched by gypsy gang forced to work in UK,' *The Telegraph* newspaper published in *The Sydney Morning Herald* newspaper, 29 September 2010.

Bolt, Andrew, 'Hunting for Eddie's racists,' *Herald Sun* newspaper, 22 July 2009.

Bolt, Andrew, 'Keeping appearances on immigration,' *Herald Sun* newspaper, 27 April 2011.

Boyer, Dave, 'Philadelphia mayor talks tough to black teenagers after 'flash mobs',' *The Washington Times* newspaper, 8 August 2011.

Brown, Malcolm, 'Policewoman attack: man refused bail,' *The Sydney Morning Herald* newspaper, 15 May 2009.

Brown, Malcolm, 'Student sues for 'Asian phobia',' *The Sydney Morning Herald* newspaper, 28 October 2008.

Burstein, Nathan, 'Google sued in France over 'Jewish' searches,' *Jewish Times* newspaper, 29 April 2012.

Butcher, Steve, 'Natasha's weapons boob: 'I need them for Springvale',' *The Age* newspaper, 15 June 2012.

Carlqvist, Ingrid and Lars Hedegaard, 'Sweden: Rape Capital of the West,' *Gatestone Institute*, 14 February 2015, citing radio station *Granskning Sverige*.

Chambers, Geoff, 'Police in Sydney to monitor rallies for the prophet Mohammed,' *The Daily Telegraph* newspaper, 20 January 2015.

Chambers, Geoff, 'Rugby league referees need lesson in culture, say experts,' *The Daily Telegraph* newspaper, 26 June 2010.

Chawla, Kiran, 'Police: Family attacked for being in 'wrong neighborhood',' *WAFB Channel 9 News Baton Rouge*, 13 May 2013.

Coles, John, 'Asylum Seeker jailed for rape,' *The Sun* newspaper, 8 January 2009.

Collier, Karen, 'Violence and bullying sweep our state schools,' *Herald Sun* newspaper, 27 October 2008. The home page introduced the article 'Class war in state schools.'

Cooper, Mex, 'Shot Tyler's 'nationalist' MySpace page,' *The Age* newspaper, 12 December 2008.

Corderoy, Amy, 'Family celebrates start of a new life,' *The Sydney Morning Herald* newspaper, 24 December 2009.

Correspondents in Grenoble, 'Rioters cause havoc in French city of Grenoble' and 'Riots erupt in French city La Villeneuve,' *Agence France-Presse* news service published at *News Limited Network*, 18 July 2010.

Corsi, Jerome, 'CDC denies enterovirus link to illegal-alien kids,'

World Net Daily, 15 October 2014.

Craw, Victoria, 'Four people stabbed on Children's Day Parade of Notting Hill Carnival,' *News Limited Network*, 30 August 2016.

Davidson, Sinclair, 'Refugee crime wave nothing but hogwash,' *Unleashed* at *Australian Broadcasting Corporation News*, 26 May 2011.

Davies, Lisa, 'Kings Cross gang muscles in on Gold Coast and Melbourne drug trade,' *The Daily Telegraph* newspaper, 17 February 2010.

Day, Lauren, 'Burmese refugee found guilty of assault,' *Australian Broadcasting Corporation News*, 4 October 2012.

De Carbonnel, Alissa and Gleb Bryanski, 'Putin warns ethnic tensions risk tearing Russia apart,' *Reuters* news service, 23 January 2012.

De Ceglie, Anthony and Nicole Cox, 'Police Union angry at 'political correctness gone mad' on naming offenders' race,' *The Sunday Times* newspaper, 27 November 2010. Anthony DeCeglie and Nicole Cox, 'WA Police defend policy on not naming offenders' race,' *The Sunday Times* newspaper, 29 November 2010.

Deacon, Liam, 'CLAIM: 'No Borders' Activist Gang Raped By Migrants, Pressured Into Silence To Not 'Damage Cause,' *Breitbart News*, 6 October 2015.

Derbyshire, John, 'The Talk: Nonblack Version,' *Taki's Magazine*, 5 April 2012. Cosby Hunt, 'Trayvon Martin: A Tragic Death and A Lesson Learned,' *National Public Radio*, 20 March 2012. Corey Dade, 'Florida Teen's Killing: A Parent's Greatest Fear,' *National Public Radio*, 21 March 2012. Guardian staff, 'National Review fires John Derbyshire over race article,' *The Guardian* newspaper, 8 April 2012.

Devine, Miranda, 'Cabramatta then, now and post-poll,' *The Sydney Morning Herald* newspaper, 11 July 2002.

Devine, Miranda, 'Racism cry is the only weapon,' *The Sydney Morning Herald* newspaper, 4 June 2009, reporting closed circuit television.

Dinan, Stephen, 'Federal authorities charge white 'knockout' suspect with hate crime,' *The Washington Times* newspaper, 26 December 2013.

Farrelly, Elizabeth, 'Racism helps to ease the whitewash of Redfern,' *The Sydney Morning Herald* newspaper, 30 July 2008.

Fewster, Sean, 'Kapunda killer Jason Downie pleads guilty,' *Adelaide Now*, 9 November 2011.

Field, Donna, '18yo fronts court over Joan Ryther's murder at Logan,' *Australian Broadcasting Corporation News*, 3 June 2013.

Fife-Yeomans, Janet, 'Australians are racist, says street thug Sam 'The Assassin',' *The Daily Telegraph* newspaper, 7 May 2009.

Fife-Yeomans, Janet, 'Thomas Kelly's family furious at Pat O'Shane over her 'incredibly offensive' remarks,' *The Daily Telegraph* newspaper, 21 September 21, 2013. Peter Bodkin, 'Thomas Kelly 'king-hit' charges may not be murder,' *Australian Associated Press* news service published at *The Daily Telegraph* newspaper, 5 June 2013.

Fife-Yeomans, Janet and Simon Black, 'Australia's Generation Jihad is homegrown,' *The Daily Telegraph* newspaper, 30 May 2013.

Gardiner, Stephanie and Nick Ralston, 'Man stabbed, bashed by gang was 'in the wrong place at the wrong time': police,' *The Sydney Morning Herald* newspaper, 5 January 2012.

Gardiner, Stephanie with Saffron Howden and *Australian Associated Press* news service, 'Another night, another drive-by shooting as Sydney house targeted,' *The Sydney Morning Herald* newspaper, August 23, 2011. Alicia Wood, 'Sydney drive-by shootings: it all started with Albert Slater,' *The Sydney Morning Herald* newspaper, 17 January 2012.

Gibson, Joel, 'Court allows police killer to stay for daughter's sake,' *The Sydney Morning Herald* newspaper, 3 December 2009.

Gillett, Bud, 'Plano Police Warn Hispanic Men of Violent Attacks,' *CBS 11 News Dallas, Fort Worth*, 22 February 2013.

Gilmore, Heath, 'Call for racial profiling to prove Australia is safe,' *The Sydney Morning Herald* newspaper, 2 June 2010.

Gridneff, Ilya, 'One street paved the way for city's notorious crimes,' *The Sydney Morning Herald* newspaper, 26 November 2012. Ilya Gridneff, 'One dead after shooting in Punchbowl,' *The Sydney Morning Herald* newspaper, 27 November 2012. Rachel Olding with others, 'Punchbowl shooting: dead man was father of four,' *The Sydney Morning Herald* newspaper, 28 November 2012.

Gridneff, Ilya, 'Supermarket 'upskirter' hid camera in shopping basket, police claim,' *The Sydney Morning Herald* newspaper, 16 March 2012.

Gutteridge, Nick, "Trump is right!' Police say parts of Britain ARE no-go areas due to ISIS radicalisation,' *Daily Express* newspaper, 9 December 2015. Uncredited, 'Communities 'taking law into their own hands', says police chief inspector,' *The Guardian* newspaper, 19 January 2014.

Hagan, Kate, 'Man 'looking to kill blacks' murdered Sudanese,' *The Sydney Morning Herald* newspaper, 1 October 2009.

Hall, Allan, 'Family of EU official's teenage daughter who was raped and killed 'by Afghan migrant' ask for well-wishers to donate money to refugee charity as teenage 'killer' is revealed,' *Daily Mail* newspaper, 6 December 2016.

Hefling, Kimberly, 'Survey: School bullying problem recedes; whites more likely targets than minorities,' *Associated Press* news service published at *Star Tribune* newspaper, 15 May 2015.

Hefling, Kimberly with Pete Yost, 'Holder's New School Discipline Guidelines: Stop Targeting Minorities,' *Breitbart News*, 8 January 2014. Warner Todd Huston, 'Minneapolis School District Now Needs 'Permission' to Suspend Any Black, Hispanic Student,' *Breitbart News*, 9 November 2014. Steve Gunn, 'Teachers complain, chaos reigns as St. Paul schools spend millions on 'white privilege' training,' *EAG news*, 2 June 2015. Paul Sperry, 'Obama collecting personal data for a secret race database,' *New York Post* newspaper, 18 July 2015.

Henderson, Gerard, 'Student assaults teach some harsh lessons about racism,' *The Sydney Morning Herald* newspaper, 5 January 2010.

Hoft, Jim, 'OPEN BORDERS ACTIVIST Beaten and Stabbed in the Back By Arab Migrants,' *The Gateway Pundit* citing *Breitbart News* and Germany's *Bild-Zeiting* newspaper, 16 October 2015.

Howden, Saffron, 'Cultural cringe: schoolchildren can't see the yoghurt for the trees,' *The Sydney Morning Herald* newspaper, 5 March 2012.

Huber, Robert, 'Being White in Philly: Whites, race, class, and the things that never get said,' *Philadelphia* magazine, March 2013. Mike Dougherty, 'Controversial Article Published in Local Magazine Has Mayor Nutter Asking for Investigation,' *CBS News Philadelphia*, 15 March 2013.

Hunt, Elissa, 'Road rage to blame for East Bentleigh crash that killed woman's unborn baby nine days ago, court hears,' *Herald Sun* newspaper, 7 January 2010.

Huston, Warner Todd, 'Suddenly Media Worried Over Reporting Race-Based Motive of Killer of White Reporters,' *Breitbart News*, 27 August 2015. Uncredited, 'Virginia shooting: Gunman fired for performance, not race, manager says, as town mourns journalists shot on-air,' *Australian Broadcasting Corporation News*, 28 August 2015. Marisa Schultz and Frank Rosario, 'The comments that became a reporter's death sentence,' *New York Post* newspaper, 28 August 2015.

Iaria, Melissa, 'Predator jailed for 'ugly, vicious' rape,' *Australian Associated Press* news service published at *News Limited Network*, 27 November 2009.

Jacobsen, Geesche, 'Call to cut Aboriginal offenders' sentences,' *The Sydney Morning Herald* newspaper, 14 December 2010. Paul Sheehan, 'Cast adrift from reality, the slick spruikers of 'our' shame,' *The Sydney Morning Herald* newspaper, 3 January 2011.

Jilani, Zaid, 'Amazon.com Is Funding Global Warming Denial in Our Schools,' *Republic Report*, 4 May 2012, mentioning Tennessee Bill HB0368.

Karimi, Faith, "Raise your voice, not your hands,' cops urge as Zimmerman verdict looms,' *Cable News Network*, 10 July 2013. Ben Shapiro, 'CNN Labels Zimmerman 'White Hispanic',' *Breitbart News*, 11 July 2013. Juan Williams, "Crackers,' a 'teenage mammy' – the sorry truth about race and Zimmerman trial,' *Fox News*, 11 July 2013.

Kennedy, Les, 'Chinatown brawl reveals new Triad-style crime gang,' *The Sydney Morning Herald* newspaper, 6 June 2010.

Kennedy, Les, 'Mayhem at Merrylands: school revenge attack,' *The Sydney Morning Herald* newspaper, 24 September 2008.

Kennedy, Les and Ellie Harvey, 'Young detective fatally shot during drug raid,' *The Sydney Morning Herald* newspaper, 9 September 2010. Uncredited, 'Philip Nguyen pleads guilty to police officer Bill Crews' manslaughter,' *The Daily Telegraph* newspaper, 19 July 2012.

Kern, Soeren, 'Police Warn of No-Go Zones in Germany,' *Gatestone Institute*, 1 August 2015.

King, Madonna, 'Political correctness has crossed the line,' *The Drum* at *Australian Broadcasting Corporation News*, 23 November 2010.

Koch, Tony, 'Aboriginal campaigner shut door to end sexual abuse,' *The Australian* newspaper, 18 May 2009.

Kontominas, Bellinda, 'Defendant must give victim $130,000,' *The Sydney Morning Herald* newspaper, 1 February 2010.

Kontominas, Bellinda, "Die bitch die': teacher sues over student's pistol threat,' *The Sydney Morning Herald* newspaper, 16 June 2010.

Kwek, Glenda, 'Two hurt in mass brawl at Sydney restaurant,' *The Sydney Morning Herald* newspaper, 23 September 2010.

Linares, Edgar, "'U' Students Want Crime Alerts to Avoid Using Racial Descriptions,' *CBS News Minnesota*, 29 January 2014.

Lloyd, Justin, 'Angry Anderson blames 'other cultures' for corrupting good old Aussie violence,' *The Daily Telegraph* newspaper, 1 March 2010.

Lockett, Jon, 'SHANGHAI-LY OFFENSIVE: Chinese airline sparks race fury after in-flight magazine tells passengers to beware of ethnic minority areas in London,' *The Sun* newspaper, 7 September 2016.

Madrid correspondents, 'Riots erupt after immigrant stabbing,' *Agence France-Presse* news service, 9 December 2008. Mail Foreign Service, 'Me and my heavies: Michelle Obama goes walkabout in Marbella after 'racist' Spaniards gaff,' *Daily Mail* newspaper, 5 August 2010.

Malik, Kenan, 'The Failure of Multiculturalism: Community Versus Society in Europe,' *Foreign Affairs* magazine, March/April 2015.

Malik, Sarah, 'HIV man admits infecting women,' *Australian Associated Press* news service published at *News Limited Network*, 6 June 2011.

Markman, Rob, 'Tyler, The Creator's Mountain Dew Ads Yanked After Racist Charges,' *Music Television MTV News*, 1 May 2013.

Masters, Roy, 'Big issue no one is game to tackle,' *The Sydney Morning Herald* newspaper, 11 April 2009.

Mawby, Nathan, 'Teen attacked with meat cleaver in St Kilda,' *Herald Sun* newspaper, 29 December 2010.

McGee, Gillian and Nathan Mawby, 'Machete attack at beauty pageant party,' *Herald Sun* newspaper, 25 April 2011. Amelia Harris and Jay Savage, 'Police officers pelted with bottles in Braybrook brawl,' *Herald Sun* newspaper, 26 April 2011. Megan Levy, 'Third brawl as street violence escalates,' *The Age* newspaper, 27 April 2011. Nino Bucci, 'Migrant leaders fear more strife,' *The Age* newspaper, 27 April 2011. Shane Green, 'Africans having to fight against 'history of failure on blackness',' *The Age* newspaper, 27 April 2011.

McGregor. Ken, 'Rapist destroyed migrant's dream,' *The Advertiser* newspaper, 2 April 2009.

McKay, Danielle, 'Model Sammi Hewitt Fought For her Life in murder-suicide', 'Love fight ends in tragedy', 'Sudanese community shocked,' and 'Victim had beauty and brains,' *Mercury* newspaper, 23 March 2011.

McKenny, Leesha and Les Kennedy, 'Cases piling up for Asian Crime Squad,' *The Sydney Morning Herald* newspaper, 16 August 2009.

Meisner, Jason and Jeremy Gorner, 'Random attacks cause concern in Chicago,' *Chicago Tribune* newspaper, 6 June 2011. Jeremy Gorner and Andy Grimm, 'Teen mobs suspected in downtown assaults,' *Chicago Tribune* newspaper, 6 June 2011. 'McCarthy: NRA, Palin a part of 'government-sponsored racism',' *Chicago WLS* radio station, 24 June 2011.

Millar, Paul, 'Man held over wife's murder,' *The Age* newspaper, 31 December 2009, concerning Chamanjot Singh. Antonia Magee and Wayne Flower, 'Eight men arrested over 'race attack' on two Indians in Swanston Street,' *Herald Sun* newspaper, 26 January 2010. Six hours later, Antonia Magee and Wayne Flower, 'Five men charged over 'race attack' on two Indians in Swanston Street,' *Herald Sun* newspaper, 26 January 2010. Elissa Hunt and Lucie van den Berg, 'No jail for youths who blinded Indian student Kanan Kharbanda,' *Herald Sun* newspaper, 1 July 2010. Adrian Lowe, 'Man jailed for van rape,' *The Age* newspaper, 25 August 2010, concerning Harjot Hundal Singh.

Millard, Robin, 'Trial for black teen's murder begins,' *The Sydney Morning Herald* newspaper, 16 November 2011.

Morri, Mark, 'NSW Government target modern gypsies, the new organised criminals in massive blitz,' *The Daily Telegraph* newspaper, 29 August 2011. Mark Morri, 'Gypsies linked to Aussie bikie gangs,' *The Daily Telegraph* newspaper, 30 August 2011.

Munro, Kelsey, 'In a small patch of land, hope reborn for Sudanese refugees,' *The Sydney Morning Herald* newspaper, 5 September 2009.

Murphy, Kerry, 'Refugee rage,' *Eureka Street* website, 27 April 2011.

Murray, Elicia, 'Bribes claim insults Chinese, says ICAC,' *The Sydney Morning Herald* newspaper, 27 May 2009.

Network writer, wires, 'Dreadlocked man a 'person of interest' in the case of missing student Hannah Graham,' *News Limited Network*, 20 September 2014.

Newcomb, Alyssa, 'Google Ad Delivery Can Show 'Racial Bias,' Says Harvard Study,' *American Broadcasting Company News*, 6 February 2013.

Nolan, Kellee, 'Girl, 13, assaulted at busy station,' *The Age* newspaper, 13 September 2010. Uncredited, 'Teen allegedly sexually assaulted at Flinders St railway station in Melbourne,' *Australian Associated Press* news service published at *News Limited Network*, 13 September 2010 included closed circuit television footage of the man to whom police wanted to speak.

O'Brien, Natalie, 'Treacherous sea claims desperate family,' *The Sydney Morning Herald* newspaper, 19 December 2010.

Olding, Rachel, 'Australian Federal Police cancel Eid dinner after backlash from Muslim community,' *The Sydney Morning Herald* newspaper, 13 July 2015.

Olding, Rachel, 'Doonside gang rape: racial tensions close to boiling point, community leaders say,' *The Sydney Morning Herald* newspaper, 12 February 2014.

Olsen, Jan, 'Gunman wounds 2 Israelis in Denmark mall shooting,' *Associated Press* news service, 31 December 2008.

Packham, Ben, 'Boat people are spreading TB and other diseases,' *The Daily Telegraph* newspaper, 12 October 2010.

Pignal, Stanley and Peggy Hollinger, 'Sarkozy rages at EU 'humiliation',' *Financial Times* newspaper, 16 September 2010.

Priestley, Andrew, 'Luke, 16, bashed by eight men after helping his mate,' *The North Shore Times* newspaper 13 October 2009.

Pronina, Lyubov, 'Medvedev Shows Off Sample Coin of New 'World Currency' at G-8,' *Bloomberg* news service, 10 July 2009.

Putin, Vladimir, 'A Plea for Caution from Russia,' *The New York Times* newspaper, 11 September 2013.

Ralston, Nick, 'Race-hate fears over fatal bashing,' *The Sydney Morning Herald* newspaper, 24 February 2010. Joel Gibson and others, 'Family held over death of wife's workmate at consulate,' *The Sydney Morning Herald* newspaper, 25 February 2010. Paul Bibby, 'Alleged murder an honour killing, court told,' *The Sydney Morning Herald* newspaper, 18 October 2011.

Ralston, Nick and Saffron Howden, 'Schoolboy arrested after playground stabbing,' *The Sydney Morning Herald* newspaper, 24

February 2011.

Ramachandran, Arjun, 'Call to end protests as another charged,' *The Sydney Morning Herald* newspaper, 11 June 2009. Arjun Ramachandran, 'Harris Park violence 'going on for years',' *The Sydney Morning Herald* newspaper, 11 June 2009.

Ramachandran, Arjun, 'Plucky youngster fights off attacker,' *The Sydney Morning Herald* newspaper, 8 August 2008.

Ravens, Tara, 'NSW laws passed to end right to silence, *Australian Associated Press* news service published at *News Limited Network*, 20 March 2013.

Reynolds, Emma, 'Ikea murders in Sweden and the refugee backlash,' *News Limited Network*, 1 October 2015.

Robinson, Georgina with others and the *Winnipeg Sun* newspaper, 'Fate turns ugly again for family that knows about pain,' *The Sydney Morning Herald* newspaper, 11 March 2010. Jodie Minus, 'Wheelchair-bound Canadian brutally bashed at Sydney train station,' *The Australian* newspaper, 10 March 2010.

Robinson, Georgina with Peter Hawkins, 'Pair in balcony plunge after being chased by intruder,' *The Sydney Morning Herald* newspaper, 27 October 2008. Dylan Welch with others, 'Balcony plunge: Sydney man charged with murder, sex assault,' *The Sydney Morning Herald* newspaper, 30 October 2008. Laura Tunstall, 'Mother of murdered student arrives to bury her only child,' *Macquarie National News*, 30 October 2008. Kim Arlington, 'Homeless man pleads guilty to balcony plunge murder,' *The Sydney Morning Herald* newspaper, 4 December 2009.

Robinson, Georgina, 'Sexual assault: woman fights off attacker with large overbite,' *The Sydney Morning Herald* newspaper, 11 May 2009.

Ross, Norrie, 'Serial rapist's Afghan ethnicity no excuse, says judge,' *Herald Sun* newspaper, 12 April 2012. Padraic Murphy, 'Afghan refugee Esmatullah Sharifi's rape sentence cut by Court of Appeal over upbringing,' *Herald Sun* newspaper, 27 May 2013.

Rubinsztein-Dunlop, Sean and staff, 'Afghan faction splits Brothers 4 Life gang, raising fears of more violence,' *Australian Broadcasting Corporation News*, 20 November 2013.

Scheikowski, Margaret, 'Father 'defamed principal', lawyer says,' *The Sydney Morning Herald* newspaper, 22 July 2009.

Siebold, Sabine, 'Merkel says German multiculturalism has failed,' *Reuters* news service, 17 October 2010. Uncredited, 'Merkel says German multicultural society has failed,' *BBC News*, 17 October 2010. Anna Reimann, 'Erdogan Escalates Germany Criticism,' *Der Spiegel* magazine, 11 February 2011.

Smajilhodzic, Rusmir, 'German girl locked up for years by Bosnian couple: police,' *Agence France-Presse* news service published at *Yahoo! News*, 27 May 2012.

Staff writers, 'Luke Mitchell dies after Brunswick bashing' and 'Luke Mitchell 'killers' flee Australia,' *Herald Sun* newspaper, 25 May 2009. Comments posted on *News Limited Network*.

Steinhauer, Jennifer, 'Korean-Americans brace for a backlash after Virginia Tech shootings,' *International Herald Tribune* newspaper, 19 April 2007. Uncredited, 'Student decapitated in same uni where massacre took place,' *Associated Press* news service, 23 January 2009. Uncredited, 'Virginia Tech found negligent over 2007 massacre,' *Associated Press* news service published at *The Sydney Morning Herald* newspaper, 15 March 2012.

Stolz, Greg and Jeremy Pierce, 'Father cautions drivers after Gold Coast road rage murder of son Omega Ruston,' *The Courier Mail* newspaper, 27 January 2009.

Swanwick, Tristan and Robyn Ironside, 'Man charged over alleged rape of girl, 14, in city lane,' *The Courier Mail* newspaper, 26 May 2009.

Tatnell, Paul, 'Sydney bashing: teen thrown off bridge,' *The Sydney Morning Herald* newspaper, 11 November 2010.

Tatnell, Paul, 'Tourist fights for life after one punch from boy as young as 10 floors him at Sydney station',' *News Limited Network*, 7 April 2010. Uncredited, 'Twin schoolboys set upon Scottish tourist in brawl, court hears,' *Australian Associated Press* news service published at *News Limited Network*, 8 April 2010.

Todd, Tony, "Misunderstanding' over Islamic art sparks near-riot,' *France 24* news service, 4 October 2012.

Tomazin, Farrah, 'Violent extremism part of contemporary Australia: Andrews,' *The Age* newspaper, 18 October 2015.

Trexler, Phil, 'Akron police investigate teen mob attack on family,' *Akron Beacon Journal* newspaper, 7 July 2009.

Uncredited, '$545m to teach migrants Aussie values (and English language),' *The Daily Telegraph* newspaper, 15 May 2015.

Uncredited, 'Ali Mobayad accused of assaulting ambo as she

treated car crash victim,' *The Daily Telegraph* newspaper, 1 April 2011.

Uncredited, 'Australia Forum,' *Topix* website, 13 May 2008, concerning Robert El-Chammas.

Uncredited, 'Boat blast men 'should not have been given visas',' *Australian Associated Press* news service published at *News Limited Network*, 12 October 2009. Dog Whistle of Bogan Island's comments were published at 2.46pm.

Uncredited, 'Bono supports 'shoot the farmer' lyrics,' *Australian Associated Press* news service published at *News Limited Network*, 13 February 2011.

Uncredited, 'Carjacking attempt on highway,' *Australian Associated Press* news service, 14 May 2009.

Uncredited, 'Chaos in Mount Druitt brawl,' *Australian Broadcasting Corporation News*, 4 February 2011. Tim Vollmer and others, 'Homies now in the big house over turf,' *The Daily Telegraph* newspaper, 5 February 2011.

Uncredited, 'Coffs Harbour rapists Silas Gordon Haines and Nathan Dungay sent to jail,' *Australian Associated Press* news service published at *News Limited Network*, 14 May 2010.

Uncredited, 'Danish man arrested over mall shooting,' *Associated Press* news service, 2 January 2009.

Uncredited, 'Eastern European gangs hit ATMs: police,' *The Sydney Morning Herald* newspaper, 29 July 2010.

Uncredited, 'Farming communities conned by gypsies,' *The Daily Telegraph* newspaper, 19 October 2008.

Uncredited, 'Food Fight Turns Into Melee At Mpls. South High,' *CBS News Minneapolis*, 14 February 2013.

Uncredited, 'Gang of up to 20 men attack teen,' *Australian Associated Press* news service published in abridged form in *The Sydney Morning Herald* newspaper, 20 February 2012. The complete *Australian Associated Press* news service report appeared at 'Man stabbed in attack by up to 20 men,' *News Limited Network*, 20 February 2012.

Uncredited, 'Gillard's Mission Improbable,' *The Sydney Morning Herald* newspaper, 10 July 2010.

Uncredited, 'Girl, 5, London's youngest gun gang victim,' *Press Association* news service published in *The Sydney Morning Herald* newspaper, 31 March 2011.

Uncredited, 'Hard-working family man paid 12-year-old girl $10 for sex act, court hears,' *Australian Associated Press* news service published at *The Sydney Morning Herald* newspaper, 25 May 2012.

Uncredited, 'Hunt for the man with the souped-up car and the blond tips in his hair, *Australian Associated Press* news service published in *The Sydney Morning Herald* newspaper, 19 July 2011.

Uncredited, "I run Bankstown': man killed teen to prove he 'owned' suburb,' *The Sydney Morning Herald* newspaper, 28 June 2013. Rachel Olding, 'Father jailed for 'vengeful' killing of Brandon Siaa at Bankstown train station,' *The Sydney Morning Herald* newspaper, 20 September 2013.

Uncredited, 'Indian students charged over train sex attack,' *Australian Associated Press* news service published at *News Limited Network*, 4 September 2009. Uncredited, 'Two on train sex charges refused bail,' *Australian Associated Press* news service published at *News Limited Network*, 4 September 2009.

Uncredited, 'International gun syndicate linked to Sydney post office,' *Australian Associated Press* news service published at *The Sydney Morning Herald* newspaper, 14 March 2012.

Uncredited, 'Kenya court finds white aristocrat guilty of manslaughter,' *Agence France-Presse* news service published in *The Sydney Morning Herald* newspaper, 8 May 2009.

Uncredited, 'Korean man who beat child dodges jail because of cultural differences,' *The Courier Mail* newspaper, 23 October 2009.

Uncredited, 'Liberals committed to 'cultural diversity',' *Australian Associated Press* news service published at *Yahoo! News*, 24 February 2011.

Uncredited, 'Libyan Almahde Ahmad Atagore jailed for string of Melbourne sex assaults,' *Australian Associated Press* news service published at *News Limited Network*, 31 May 2011.

Uncredited, 'Maim at random: teen jailed for meat cleaver attack,' *Australian Associated Press* news service published at the *Sydney Morning Herald* newspaper, 25 May 2010.

Uncredited, 'Malmö shaken by another grenade attack,' *TT, The Local, Sweden*, 10 August 2015.

Uncredited, 'Man charged over Melbourne 'hit-run',' *Australian Associated Press* news service published at the *Herald Sun* newspaper, 13 August 2013.

Uncredited, 'Man ignores teen's rape in flowerbed,' *Australian Associated Press* news service published in *the Sydney Morning*

Herald newspaper, 12 July 2011.

Uncredited, 'Man injured in savage golf club attack,' *Australian Associated Press* news service, 21 July 2010.

Uncredited, 'Man offers cash in latest kidnap attempt,' *Australian Associated Press* news service, 12 October 2008.

Uncredited, 'Married killer lured girlfriend to death,' *Australian Associated Press* news service, 22 April 2009.

Uncredited, 'Murdered for 'staring' in CBD: killer gets 19 years,' *Australian Associated Press* news service published in *The Sydney Morning Herald* newspaper, 18 June 2010.

Uncredited, 'Nephew of Somalian dictator avoids jail over sex assault,' *Australian Associated Press* news service published in *The Sydney Morning Herald* newspaper, 7 June 2010.

Uncredited, "Non-existent' crime worries Aussies,' *Australian Associated Press* news service published in *The Chronicle* (Toowoomba) newspaper, 26 May 2009.

Uncredited, 'NT schools are safe, despite stabbing,' *Australian Associated Press* news service published at *News Limited Network*, 23 March 2011.

Uncredited, 'Pitched battle at beauty pageant,' *Australian Associated Press* news service published at *The Sydney Morning Herald* newspaper, 4 October 2010. Jason Pobjoy, 'We can do more to give child refugees a home, *The Sydney Morning Herald* newspaper, 4 October 2010. Amy Noonan, 'Police hunt for carjacker,' *Adelaide Now*, 4 October 2010

Uncredited, 'Police investigate schoolgirl assaults,' *Australian Associated Press* news service, 21 July 2010. Uncredited, 'Girls' attacker eludes police,' *The Sydney Morning Herald* newspaper, 27 July 2010.

Uncredited, 'Poster contest spreads Harmony Day message,' *The Sydney Morning Herald* newspaper, 8 August 2011.

Uncredited, 'Racial profiling OK for defence staff,' *Australian Associated Press* news service published at *News Limited Network*, 19 January 2011.

Uncredited, 'Racism 'does exist in Australia',' *Australian Associated Press* news service published at *News Limited Network*, 14 June 2009.

Uncredited, 'Racist who plotted tennis ball bombings convicted,' *The Sydney Morning Herald* newspaper, 16 July 2009.

Uncredited, 'Refugees beat Buckley's chance,' *The Sydney Morning*

Herald newspaper, 27 September 2008. *Deutsche Presse Agentur*, 'Bloomberg Suspects seized at airport,' *The Sydney Morning Herald* newspaper, 27 September 2008.

Uncredited, 'Riots grip Stockholm suburbs after police shooting,' *BBC News*, 22 May 2013. Uncredited, 'Sweden riots spread to south of capital,' *Bloomberg* news service published in the *Irish Times* newspaper, 23 May 2013. Uncredited, "They don't want to integrate': Fifth night of youth rioting rocks Stockholm, *TV – Nosti*, RT network, 23 and 24 May 2013. Colin Freeman in Husby, 'Stockholm riots leave Sweden's dreams of perfect society up in smoke,' *The Telegraph* newspaper, 25 May 2013. Editorial, 'Sweden: reading the riots,' *The Guardian* newspaper, 27 May 2013.

Uncredited, 'Teenage boy thwarts abduction attempt,' *Australian Associated Press* news service published in *The Sydney Morning Herald* newspaper, 3 September 2010.

Uncredited, 'Teenage girl escapes abductor,' *Australian Associated Press* news service, 4 October 2008.

Uncredited, 'Thi Truong Tran and Manh Dao face court over $44m drug bust,' *Australian Associated Press* news service published at *News Limited Network*, 14 July 2011.

Uncredited, 'UK jails woman for racist rant on London subway,' *Associated Press* news service, 29 May 2012. Uncredited, 'Racist Tube rant woman Jacqueline Woodhouse jailed,' *BBC News*, 29 May 2012.

Uncredited, 'Yanna Fang's family condemned to 'lifetime sentence of endless sorrow',' *Australian Associated Press* news service published in *The Sydney Morning Herald* newspaper, 21 July 2010.

Wade, Matt, "Racist Australia' was grist for India's media mill,' *The Sydney Morning Herald* newspaper, 4 July 2009. Rick Wallace, 'Killing of student Nitin Garg threatens ties: India,' *The Australian* newspaper, 4 January 2010. Nick O'Malley, 'Killing reveals another kind of race problem,' *The Sydney Morning Herald* newspaper, 8 January 2010, quoting *Times Now* in India. Lauren Wilson and Amanda Hodge, 'Time for rethink on race issue in Indian deaths,' *The Australian* newspaper, 11 March 2010. Uncredited, 'Second arrest in Indian student's murder,' *The Australian* newspaper, 18 June 2010. Peter Lalor, 'Ugly, ugly, ugly say India's media,' *The Australian* newspaper, 8 October 2010.

Wallace, Natasha, 'Nice little earner, but pity the workers,' *The Sydney Morning Herald* newspaper, 17 September 2011.

Washington, Michelle, 'A beating at Church and Brambleton,' *Virginian-Pilot* newspaper, 1 May 2012. Kovacs, '100 blacks beat white couple, media bury attack,' *World News Daily* website, 1 May 2012.

Welch, Dylan, 'Auburn riot fears halt raids, police say,' *The Sydney Morning Herald* newspaper, 16 November 2009.

Welch, Dylan with others, 'Not even a bystander, but a victim of random madness,' *The Sydney Morning Herald* newspaper, 27 June 2009. Alison Rehn and David Barrett, 'KFC gunfight bullet kills a loving father,' *The Daily Telegraph* newspaper, 27 June 2009.

Wood, Alicia, 'Brothers charged with 20 child sex offences,' *The Sydney Morning Herald* newspaper, 11 July 2010.

Woodcock, Andrew, 'Hate crimes aimed at Muslims to get own category, bringing Islamophobia in line with anti-Semitism,' *The Independent* newspaper, 13 October 2015.

Wright, Anne, 'Car thieves release handbrakes to allow cars to roll into poles, fences and signs in Melbourne's east,' *Herald Sun* newspaper, 8 June 2010.

Zielinski, Caroline and others, 'Mustafa Kunduraci charged with murder of Moonee Ponds couple,' *Australian Associated Press* news service published in *The Age* newspaper, 10 December 2013.

Books

Cameron, Averil, born 1940, *The Later Roman Empire AD 284-430* (1993), Harvard University Press. Ben Wilkie, 'What do we really think about immigrants?' *The Drum* at *Australian Broadcasting Corporation News*, 10 October 2011, with comment by Observer.

Dawkins, Richard, born 1941, *The Selfish Gene* (1976).

Eagleman, David, *Incognito: The Secret Lives of the Brain* (2011). David Eagleman, 'The Brain on Trial,' *Atlantic* magazine, July/August 2011.

Einstein, Albert, 1879-1955, *Relativity: The Special and the General Theory* (1916).

Freedman, Jane, *Immigration and Insecurity in France* (2004) Ashgate Publishing. Pages 35 and 36 referred to the French government's *aide au retour* (help to return), announced in 1977.

King, Martin Luther, 1929-1968, *Strength to Love* (1963).

Mazari, Najaf and Robert Hillman, *The Rugmaker of Mazar-e-Sharif* (2008), Wild Dingo, reviewed by Julian Burnside.

Mill, John Stuart, 1806-1873, *Representative Government*, Chapter XVI (1859).

Raine, Adrian, *The Anatomy of Violence: The Biological Roots of Crime* (2013). Tim Adams, 'How to spot a murderer's brain,' *The Observer* newspaper, 12 May 2013. Jari Tiihonen, and others, 'Genetic background of extreme violent behavior,' *Molecular Psychiatry*, 28 October 2014. Uncredited, 'Are murderers born or made?' *BBC* magazine, 9 March 2015. Sherine Conyers, 'Australian convict history could mean 'warrior gene' leaves a legacy of crime in our blood,' *News Limited Network*, 21 March 2015.

Russell, Bertrand, 1872-1970, *A History of Western Philosophy* (1945), Simon and Schuster. Words from page 772 were quoted in the *Molong Express* newspaper, 19 May 2011, page 11.

Films

Applicant, The. Connie Levett, 'Finding a boss who sees more than your skin,' *The Sydney Morning Herald* newspaper, 4 February 2008.

Colour Blind. Connie Levett, 'Finding a boss who sees more than your skin,' *The Sydney Morning Herald* newspaper, 4 February 2008.

Harry Potter and the Half-Blood Prince (2009), based upon the 2005 novel by J.K. Rowling, born 1965. Paul Sims, 'Mother-of-two who told thugs to be quiet in Harry Potter film left seriously burnt after bleach attack,' *Daily Mail* newspaper, 31 July 2009, published as 'Harry Potter movie-goer doused in bleach,' *News Limited Network*, 31 July 2009.

Jurassic Park (1993), based upon the 1990 novel by Michael Crichton, 1942-2008. Rhodri Phillips, 'You're the Jong that I want,' *The Sun* newspaper, 9 April 2013.

Mississippi Burning (1988), written by Chris Gerolmo.

Judgments

Brown v Board of Education of Topeka 347 U.S. 483 (1954).

Bugmy v The Queen [2013] HCA 37 (2 October 2013). Gordon Taylor, 'Indigenous disadvantage does not diminish over time, High Court rules,' *Australian Broadcasting Corporation News*, 2 October 2013.

Savage, James Hudson v State of Florida [1992] Aboriginal LB 39.

Swann v Charlotte-Mecklenburg Board of Education 402 U.S. 1 (1971).

Reports

Dunn, Kevin, and others, University of Western Sydney, *Challenging Racism: The Anti-Racism Research Project*, 2008. Uncredited, '40pc believe others don't belong here,' *Australian Associated Press* news service, 28 September 2008.

Songs

'Imagine' (1971), by John Lennon, 1940-1980. Uncredited, 'Lennon was a closet Republican: Assistant,' *Toronto Sun* newspaper, 28 June 2011, citing the documentary *Beatles Stories* from Seth Swirsky.

'Sniper' (1972), from the album *Sniper and Other Love Songs* (1972), by Harry Chapin, 1942-1981.

Television Programmes

Can Of Worms (2011-2013, especially 18 July 2011), Ten Network Australia. Uncredited, 'John Elliott offends on Can of Worms,' *The Age* newspaper, 19 July 2011.

Cheers (1982-1993), with John Ratzenberger playing Cliff Clavin. Staff, 'Cheers' Star – My Ex Might Set My Car on Fire,' *Thirty Mile Zone* website, 13 May 2009.

Fawlty Towers (1975, 1979), especially the episode 'The Anniversary' (1979).

Go Back to Where You Came From (2011), Australian Broadcasting Corporation.

Mad Dog: Inside the Secret World of Muammar Gaddafi (2014). Lawrence Dunhill, 'Lecturer tells of when Gaddafi studied in

Beaconsfield,' *Bucks Free Press*, 2 March 2011.

Once Upon a Time in Cabramatta, (broadcast 8 January 2012), Special Broadcasting Service. Andrew Jakubowicz, 'From war to tough new frontier: the Vietnamese path to cohesion,' *The Sydney Morning Herald* newspaper, 7 January 2012.

Power Games (2013), Channel Nine, Australia.

Sesame Street (1969 onwards).

Weg van Nederland (2011), public broadcaster RNW. Peter Walker, 'Dutch gameshow pits failed asylum seekers against each other,' *The Guardian* newspaper, 1 September 2011.

ABOUT THE AUTHOR

Simon Lennon has travelled throughout Europe, America, Australasia, Asia, and the South Pacific, seeing how similar European peoples are to each other (wherever we live) and how different we of the West are to everyone else. He has university bachelor's degrees in science and law and university master's degrees in commerce and business. He is married with six children.

His non-fiction collection *The West* comprises the following sixteen books:

Mending the West
The Unnatural West: An Overview
The Tribeless West: An Overview
The Homeless West: An Overview
The Vanishing West: An Overview

Individualism
Western Individualism
The End of Natural Selection
The Need for Nations

Identity
People's Identity: Race and Racism
Of Whom We're Born: Race and Family
Biological Us: Gender and Sexuality

Nationalism
A Land to Belong: Nationalism
The Failure of Multiculturalism

Cultures
Reclaiming Western Cultures
Christendom Lost
Aiding Islam

He is also the author of another non-fiction book, two collections of short stories, and five novels.

www.ingramcontent.com/pod-product-compliance
Lightning Source LLC
Chambersburg PA
CBHW020002290326
41935CB00007B/268